W9-BXE-304

we all wore stars

we all wore stars

Memories of Anne Frank from Her Classmates

Theo Coster

Translated from the Dutch by
Marjolijn de Jager

The translation of the book was supported by a grant from the Dutch Foundation for Literature.

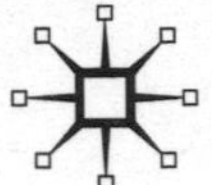

First published in the Netherlands as *Klasgenoten van Anne Frank* by Uitgeverij Carrera, Amsterdam.

First published in English in 2011 by PALGRAVE MACMILLAN® in the United States–a division of St. Martin's Press LLC, 175 Fifth Avenue, New York, NY 10010.

Where this book is distributed in the UK, Europe and the rest of the world, this is by Palgrave Macmillan, a division of Macmillan Publishers Limited, registered in England, company number 785998, of Houndmills, Basingstoke, Hampshire RG21 6XS.

Palgrave Macmillan is the global academic imprint of the above companies and has companies and representatives throughout the world.

ISBN: 978-0-230-11444-9

Library of Congress Cataloging-in-Publication Data

Coster, Theo.
[Klasgenoten van Anne Frank. English]
We all wore stars : memories of Anne Frank from her classmates / by Theo Coster ; translated from the Dutch by Marjolijn de Jager.
p. cm.
ISBN 978-0-230-11444-9 (hardback)
1. Coster, Theo. 2. Jews, German—Netherlands—Amsterdam—Biography. 3. Holocaust, Jewish (1939–1945)—Netherlands—Amsterdam. 4. Frank, Anne, 1929–1945—Friends and associates. 5. Amsterdam (Netherlands)—Ethnic relations. I. Title.
DS135.N6C67313 2011
940.53'18092—dc22
[B]

2011009828

A catalogue record of the book is available from the British Library.

Design by Letra Libre

First edition: October 2011

10 9 8 7 6 5 4 3 2 1

Printed in the United States of America.

Dedicated to Suus and Barend van Beek,
who took me into their home and into their hearts
during two and a half years of World War II,
thereby seriously risking their own lives.

contents

Six pages of black-and-white photographs appear between pages 110 and 111.

acknowledgments

My heartfelt gratitude goes to those who helped me in making the documentary and writing this book—first, of course, to my former classmates Nanette Blitz (São Paulo), Hannah Goslar (Jerusalem), Lenie Duyzend (Amsterdam), Jacqueline van Maarsen (Amsterdam), and Albert Gomes de Mesquita (Eindhoven). Thanks go to my wife, Ora Rosenblat, for her love, patience, and ideas. My gratitude also goes to Eyal Boers and Martijn Kalkhoven, Uri Ackerman, Michael Goorevich, Hila Haramati, and Aliza Coster for their wonderful cooperation on the documentary; to Peter Wingender and Ronald Koopmans for their fine guidance of the documentary project in the Netherlands; to Sascha de Wied and Maurice Smirck for their advice on historical and Jewish expressions; to Harold de Croon for his confidence in publishing this book; to Annette Lavrijsen for her editorship; and to Martien Bos for putting my story down on paper.

—*Theo Coster*

translator's acknowledgments

As translator, I would like to express my deep appreciation to Theo Coster, his former classmates, and Palgrave Macmillan for bringing these stories to the public so that the next generations can always remember what must never be repeated. My gratitude also goes to my husband, David Vita, for being my first and most supportive reader.

In addition, this translation is dedicated to the memory of my late mother's dearest friend, Jean Mesritz, a Leiden University law student and a member of the Dutch Resistance who was betrayed and deported and who later died in the camp of Neuengamme in March 1945.

—MdJ

prologue

The Birth of an Idea

The time that I, fourteen-year-old Maurice Coster, spent playing with my classmates, including Anne Frank, recedes further in my memory with each passing year. It's now been more than sixty-five years since the German occupation of the Netherlands, when all Jewish children in Amsterdam were forced to attend special schools. Like Anne's parents, mine, too, selected the Jewish lyceum. As Jews were being persecuted throughout the country, more and more students disappeared from our classroom—they had either been rounded up, sent to the camps, or gone into hiding.

Thanks to my father's timely intervention, my family went into hiding before the Germans came knocking on our door. A few months earlier, my sister, three years older than me, had been sent to a Catholic boarding school for girls in Belgium. My father, my mother, and I were each hidden from the Germans in different locations in the Netherlands. I stayed in the town of Vaassen with a family that had no children, where I pretended to be a nephew from Amsterdam who had come to spend time with them. Because of my new identity, I had to come up with a different first name. I picked Theo—Theo Coster, a name that I've held onto ever since.

In retrospect, I made it through the war relatively unscathed. The rest of my family survived as well, and when we returned to Amsterdam, we were able to move right back into our old house. There it stood, in one piece, as if nothing had happened.

After the war, the only thing I wanted to do was get on with my life. In 1948, when I read *Het achterhuis*—the original Dutch title of Anne Frank's diary, meaning "The Secret Annex"—the hardships my former classmate had endured made a deep impression on me. I thought her writing, though, and actions were extraordinarily mature for someone her age.

After finishing my studies at Nyenrode Business University, I had no option but to work for my father's printing business for three years. But when I heard about the opportunities in Israel for educated young men like myself, I bought a moped in Friesland

and took off straight across Europe—a continent still recovering even as it prepared for the Cold War.

I left it all behind. In Israel, I soon found a job and met Ora, my future wife. Both she and I were Jewish and lived in Tel Aviv—where we still live today and which had become a haven for many Jews. However, I had not moved to Israel because it was a Jewish state; I was looking for a place to live and work—somewhere to be creative. That was possible for me there. Together, Ora and I soon had fantastic ideas. Our big break came in 1979 when we developed a board game we called *Wie is het?* in Dutch. The toy manufacturer Milton Bradley was as enthusiastic as we were and produced the game in Great Britain under the name *Guess Who?* It met with amazing success, was launched in the United States in 1982, and has since been sold in almost every country around the world.

THE WAR NEVER ENTIRELY VANISHED from my thoughts, but it was not until much later that I was forced to confront it all over again. *Absent: Memories of the Jewish Lyceum in Amsterdam,* a book by Dienke Hondius, was published in 2001. It gave particular emphasis to the years 1941–1943, when the noted intellectuals Jacques Presser and Jaap Meijer were on the faculty of the lyceum. As many alumni of the school as possible were invited to the book's release party. Naturally, I accepted. Ora and I were traveling all over the world for our work, and we still quite regularly visited relatives in Amsterdam. Half of the school's 110 surviving students were supposed to be there. We all waited in a small reception area at city hall for the event to begin. I didn't know what had become of my former classmates. I looked around carefully, trying to recognize in the elderly faces around me the children with whom I'd shared classes. I barely recognized a soul.

When the speeches were over, I stared aimlessly into space for a while and for a brief moment, my thoughts returned to the summer of 1944.

It's a beautiful day, and the reeds on the banks of the Apeldoorn Canal sway gently in the wind. I can barely conceal the delicious, nervous, excited feeling that I'm about to do something that's not allowed. The man with whom I'm spending the day has made me promise to keep our adventure secret.

"Put that fishing pole away," he says. He gives me a knowing look, one man to another, although I'm only fifteen. "I've got something better."

The water flows before us.

"Now take a step back," the man says as he takes something out of his shoulder bag. "Are you ready?"

I stand back expectantly, my hands covering my ears. I feel as if I'm going to get a pleasant surprise, the first one in a very long time. I can see the man's mouth moving, saying something like "There we go!" followed by my name—or what he believes to be my name, at least. With a sharp tug, he pulls the pin from a grenade, which he throws into the canal some distance from us. A split second later, a column of water erupts with a muted but forceful explosion, flying in every direction.

He looks at me and laughs. I'm in stitches. Am I nervous? There he stands, his sleeves wet, holding a net, his hands filled with the fish we'll be having for dinner tonight. The fish are shimmering in the sun, just like his boots, which have droplets of river water running down them. Even on a day like this, his boots are polished to lethal perfection, ready for the next parade. His sword belt divides his uniform into two separate sections.

As he bends down to put the fish in his bag, the sun shines directly onto the two small lightning bolts on his collar—the same letter twice, a symbol that in future decades would never lose any of its horror.

"Are you coming?"

Ora put a hand on my shoulder. I slowly cast off the memory of fifty-seven years ago. Everyone was gradually getting up from their chairs—that's how it goes at our autumnal age—or else already shuffling in the direction of a table with coffee and cake. With a few exceptions, I still didn't recognize anyone, although surely there had to be faces there that I used to see every day—faces of children who had been my classmates, with whom I'd biked to school, celebrated birthdays, and eaten ice cream. During the presentation, they, too, must have relived memories of the war years, just as I had. It occurred to me that a unique group of survivors was gathered here. A few classes overflowing with memories. I also realized that we were all close to eighty years old.

After the birth of my grandchildren, I'd become a regular visitor to school classrooms to tell my story. Israel was created to offer a safe place for the Jewish people after the horrors of the Second World War, and the recording and recounting of their experiences continues to be deeply valued there. That is why in the spring of 1951, Yom HaShoah (Holocaust day) was conceived—an annual day when the six million Jews murdered during the war are remembered. Long ago, I told my two sons how I made it through the war and that I'd been one of Anne Frank's classmates. My stories made their way to the classrooms of my grandchildren, and so one Yom HaShoah, I was asked to come and talk about my experiences and what it was like to be a friend of Anne Frank's.

The children responded very positively and were truly interested in hearing about a life that was completely unfamiliar to them. The following year, a different school invited me, and then again the next year, until I was appearing regularly.

One day in 2007, I came home and told my wife that all the lectures were becoming a bit too much for me.

"No wonder," Ora said. "You're almost eighty."

"But I feel it's my duty to keep telling my story," I said.

We sat down at the counter in our house, as we always do in trying times. We were silent for a while until Ora suddenly spoke:

"Why don't you make your story into a film?"

I looked at her in surprise. "What do you mean?"

"Why not record your story on film?" she said. "We could even turn it into a real project and enlist an interviewer and a cameraman."

I gave it some thought. It was an interesting possibility. My story would be recorded and would probably reach a larger audience than the classes I now visited once a year.

"Would it be possible to find other classmates from that time?" Ora asked. "Perhaps they'd like to collaborate and tell their stories as well."

"Anne Frank's classmates," I said.

We began to explore the idea. Six years earlier, at the book party for *Absent,* I had reconnected with my former classmate Nanette Blitz Konig, and since then, we'd kept in touch by email. She'd told me she had remained in contact with other students. I could ask her what she thought of the idea.

I looked at Ora. Since the sixties, we'd worked on all kinds of projects together; we'd invented games and made works of art, written books, painted, and done clay modeling. Why not make a film—a film about Anne Frank's classmates?

IT TURNED OUT TO BE A FRUITFUL PLAN. I spoke at great length with Nanette via Skype. Although she lived in São Paulo and I in Tel Aviv, it seemed as if we were next door to each other. We were amazed at how well we still spoke Dutch after all these years abroad. Nanette was thrilled with the idea and told me she had the contact information of four of our classmates: Jacqueline van Maarsen, Lenie Duyzend, Albert Gomes de Mesquita, and Hannah Goslar. The latter, Nanette said, was living in Jerusalem and would probably be the easiest to start with. We soon found a professional filmmaker who was also an old family acquaintance and an obvious choice: Eyal Boers, a gifted director who spoke three languages. Eyal's great-grandmother and my grandmother had played together in 1872 as little girls in Amsterdam's Weesperstraat district, and the families had remained close throughout the years.

During the months that followed, Ora and I figured out what the documentary should include. In her diary, with precision and brilliance, Anne Frank had recorded her story up to her capture. It is an extraordinary book, but it's also the story of one single Jewish girl who was forced to go into hiding. Every classmate would, of course, have his or her own unique story. Each of us had gone through such different experiences, but the Jewish lyceum was something we all shared. It seemed like a good idea to visit all those who wanted to participate and then, ideally, bring them together in Amsterdam. We would be able to share our personal experiences, as well as the collective story of a group of students whose lives had been radically changed because of the war. We could show how bad luck and good fortune are often intertwined, especially in difficult times. We would be able to record our story for future generations, just as Anne Frank had done.

At our age, time moves quickly, and the number of eyewitnesses to the Holocaust is constantly shrinking. This is one more reason to take the recording of these experiences seriously, as there are too many people today who say that this period wasn't all that awful, or worse: that the Holocaust never took place.

part 1

A New School

(Age Thirteen)

In September 1941, the Germans issued a law stipulating that Jewish and gentile children in the Netherlands were no longer allowed to attend school together. Although I had already passed the entrance exam for a public high school, I now had to attend the Jewish lyceum.

The lyceum was located on the former Stadstimmertuin, a little street very close to the Carré Theater. This high school had an all-Jewish faculty and was attended only by Jewish children. Today, the building is used as a beauty and hairdressing school, but from the outside, it still looks almost entirely the same. A warped metal Star of David above the entrance and a glass commemorative plaque are the only reminders of its history.

The school was open for just a few years. At a certain point, there simply weren't enough teachers or students left for it to operate. I was one of the students who was forced to stop early on.

During the publication event for *Absent,* it had been gratifying to see the rather large number of former students still alive. Fifty percent of the students of the lyceum survived the war, while throughout the Netherlands, only about 20 percent of Jews survived. Nobody has been able to explain the difference with any certainty, and no systematic research has (yet) been done on the question. It is assumed that many of the teachers and students managed to survive by going into hiding, as they often had the ability to pay for it. Thanks to individual contacts with the city's Jewish Council, some had been granted deportation extensions as late as 1943. Class, money, and social networks may have also all played a role. Who knows how much I owe to my father's stamp collection, which he sold off piece by piece, or to my mother's jewelry, which she sold clandestinely somewhere along the line. To some extent, it helped to have wealth or connections and friends to draw on.

Attending the lyceum gave us a sense of belonging to a special group, and that was good—

exciting, even—but at the same time, it was cause for alarm. We knew we were "chosen" for special treatment but hadn't a clue what that treatment might be. Perhaps some of the students' parents were more concretely aware, but I have the feeling they were careful not to scare their children unnecessarily. Not a single one of us had the slightest notion of what was in store.

Just before the school year began in September 1941, I had my bar mitzvah—the ceremony for a Jewish boy when he reaches his thirteenth birthday and thus, his "religious majority." The rite is often performed in a synagogue. I celebrated my bar mitzvah in a synagogue on Lek Street (the building is still there, although it no longer serves as a synagogue). At the time, the oppression of Dutch Jews didn't seem overwhelming yet—certainly not enough to prevent us from having a party. We had invited some twenty guests. I received books on chemistry (my great passion), and my mother baked a cake.

The faculty at the lyceum was not only extremely competent, but very nice as well. Jaap Meijer, my history teacher, would later become the editor of the newspaper *De Joodse wachter* (The Jewish guardian). The famed Dutch writer Jacques Presser was another beloved teacher. I didn't have any favorite subjects in particular, though I did especially well with math and the exact sciences: chemistry, physics, geometry, and algebra.

Today, I don't think of the lyceum as a "Jewish school," but rather just as a regular school attended by Jews. We didn't often pay much attention to our faith, and when we did, it was with so little fanfare that I don't remember it at all. Nor do I remember any religious instruction or specific ceremonies. I hadn't been raised Orthodox, so I didn't miss any of it.

Neither can I recall that my classmates and I spoke very much about our faith or our Jewish heritage, even though that was the very reason for our being together. We probably didn't discuss it at school because the subject received plenty of attention at home. There, we had many discussions about Judaism, but more specifically about restrictions the Germans were imposing on us. It was primarily away from home and the school that they harassed us, and we kept these conversations behind closed doors.

One day, a few children didn't show up to class. That's how simply it all began. The next day, someone else was gone. Slowly, gradually, the classrooms emptied out. Students changed their seats just to remain close to one another. No one dared ask out loud where the other children were—one way or another, we knew that this subject was taboo in the classroom.

They were absent and we didn't want to—we didn't *dare*—know anything further. Arrested or in hiding—who could tell? The only thing we knew for sure was that the students weren't absent because they were sick, and that it might have something to do with the labor camps in Germany. I myself had never seen a roundup, but I knew they happened. Adult Jews had been periodically summoned for this purpose, and from the spring of 1942 on, children barely sixteen years of age started to be included. That is how the then-sixteen-year-old Margot Frank, Anne's older sister, was called up, which convinced the Frank family to go into hiding.

It was during this same period that my parents also decided to take our family underground. I would have to go into hiding and would no longer attend school. I, too, would appear in the absentee notebook without anyone knowing what was wrong with me or where I was.

I was forced to leave before Anne Frank. At the time, she was just one of my many classmates and hadn't made a particular impression on me, although I did like her—not in a romantic sense, as I wasn't old enough for a serious relationship, nor, I think, was anyone else in our class. There may have been some youthful swooning, but no official "going steady," kissing, or more advanced amorous practices. In those days, it was quite a big deal to even walk together holding hands.

I still have a hard time calling her Anne. In our class, she was simply Annelies, the name by which she was known to everyone. It seems that she herself preferred Anne. It's the name she used in her diary and what appeared on the cover of the published edition. Be that as it may, in class it was "Annelies," and that's what I've always called her. Likewise, she never could have known that my name would become Theo later on. To her I was Maurice.

A total of 490 boys and girls had attended the Jewish lyceum, only half of whom returned after the war. My class, 1L2, had thirty students, seventeen of whom were killed in the Nazi concentration camps. Today eight live in the Netherlands, two live in Israel, and one lives in Brazil; the locations of the last two are unknown.

THE FIRST CLASSMATE I'M GOING to look up is Hannah Pick-Goslar, who lives in Israel. The drive to her house in Jerusalem is not quite sixty kilometers (thirty-five miles). Normally, it takes less than an hour to get to Jerusalem, but it's a terribly hot day and the traffic is bad. Despite the attention that the driving requires, I'm trying to review Hannah's history with Eyal, the film director. I know that she moved with her parents from Berlin to Amsterdam before the war broke out in the Netherlands. She and her whole family were arrested during the great roundup in Amsterdam-South on June 20, 1943. Hannah ended up in the Bergen-Belsen concentration camp. There, across a barbed-wire fence, she had a few brief conversations with Anne Frank. The first time she spoke with Anne was through a certain Mrs. Daan, a friend of the Frank family, who could see over the fence and tell Hannah that Anne was with her. Having assumed that Anne and her family were safely in Switzerland, Hannah couldn't believe Mrs. Daan. But then she heard Anne's voice. They were unable to see each other because the fence was lined with straw. But after they spoke with each other for a short while, Hannah promised her she'd throw a Red Cross package over the barbed wire, for on her side of the fence—which held the exchange prisoners—the captives would occasionally receive small relief packages. The following evening, she threw a package, but someone else caught it and quickly took off. A few days later, she tried again and succeeded.

Today, I want to discuss the small things with Hannah—the little things we used to do like every other child our age. I'm also curious to know her memories of our time at the lyceum.

Once we arrive, the stress of the trip quickly fades away. Hannah is a cheerful woman, with red lipstick, a red blouse, and a charming little white hat. She has a brimming bookcase and an apartment that's as bright as it is colorful—she still thoroughly enjoys life, despite her age. The sun shines sharply on the windowpanes and filters through the lace curtains, bathing the living room with light. We have cookies and drink lemonade as if Hannah has decided it will help us reminisce.

On her bookcase, I see an old edition of Anne's *Tales from the Secret Annex.* I take it out and open it. "Do you know that I'm mentioned here?" I ask. I look for the short chapter on the lyceum and read out loud the section that includes my name. Surprised, Hannah laughs: she hadn't known. Of course, everybody who was a classmate of Anne's and survived the war owns everything she ever wrote and has read all of it at least once—but that doesn't mean we know it all by heart.

With her index finger, Hannah pushes her glasses into their proper position and reads me a passage from Anne's diary. It comes from the entry of Saturday, November 27, 1943. Anne has a dream, a nightmare, about Hannah: "I saw her before me, dressed in rags, her face thin and worn out. Her eyes were very large and she looked at me so sadly and with such reproach that what I read in her eyes was: 'Oh Anne, why have you deserted me?'"

Very briefly, Hannah tenses but keeps on reading. Anne describes how guilty she feels and hopes that God will bring her solace. Anne could not know where Hannah was at that moment, because most news from the outside didn't reach the Secret Annex. "I mustn't go on thinking about it," Anne's entry continues, "because it doesn't get me anywhere. I just keep seeing her great big eyes, and can't free myself from them."

With poise, Hannah closes her copy of the book. She seems to be deciding whether to return it to the bookcase right away, and then places it on the table between us. Suddenly, the cookies and lemonade seem less convivial.

I remember that in elementary school, I had to ask my mother's permission to invite Anne to our house. Of course, that's not unusual for children of that age, but also at play at that time was the divide between Dutch Jews and Jews who came from the east.

My family had been in the Netherlands for generations, and although my mother came from Brussels, her family was from Den Bosch, in the southern part of the country. More than likely, we were descendants of Portuguese Jews, who could have been named Castro or Da Costa. It is likely that at some point, our name had been given a more Dutch-sounding form, or perhaps a distant ancestor had actually been a *koster* (a sexton). All the same, in our family, no one spoke Yiddish, which was more typical of the *Ostjuden*, the Jews from eastern Germany and Poland. Many of them had gone to the Netherlands seeking refuge from the Nazis. They naturally encountered problems there: they had been forced to abandon friends and colleagues against their will, they spoke no Dutch, and they had to find new work. In addition, many people looked down on them, considering them less civilized. However, Anne wasn't from eastern Germany but from Frankfurt: asking my mother for permission was merely a formality. I knew her the way all our classmates knew each other: we rode our bikes to school together and invited one another to birthday parties.

I say to Hannah, "In her diary, Anne writes something about a birthday party at her house. Do you remember that I was also invited to their place on the Merwedeplein?"

"Hmm," she responds after thinking it over. "To be honest, I don't recall any boys there at all."

"I really was there, though: 1942."

"Ah, wait . . . the party in 1942 when we watched that film!"

"Exactly—that's when Otto showed *Rin Tin Tin*."

"Oh yes, something's coming back to me now. Maybe they'd invited a lot of people because going to the movies was forbidden then. And perhaps that's why she invited boys as well. Because she always had many boyfriends."

"Yes, no shortage of those. Or, how did Anne herself put it? 'I have a slew of admirers who adore me and, when nothing else is feasible, try to get a glimpse of me in class with a broken pocket mirror.' Saturday, June 20, 1942. It's right here."

The party of Anne's to which I'd been invited was a daytime event at the house of the Frank family on the Merwedeplein on, maybe, a Saturday afternoon. All the kids who'd been invited were looking forward to seeing the movie *Rin Tin Tin,* a film about a heroic German shepherd—a kind of predecessor to *Lassie.*

Otto Frank worked for Opekta, a brand of pectin, which in those days was an essential ingredient for making jam. Before showing *Rin Tin Tin,* he played a short film about the uses of pectin, which I found interesting because my mother made her own strawberry jam.

There was no Coca-Cola, but we had lemonade, and there were cookies and a cake. Anne was quite popular, so there were a lot of boys and girls. She displayed her presents on a table. I don't recall what I gave her—probably a book.

"How would you describe Anne?" I ask Hannah.

"She was like pepper," she answers. "In Holland, I think you'd probably call her a know-it-all. My mother always said, 'God knows everything, but Anne knows everything better.' And I believe that Anne truly thought she knew everything better." Hannah laughs.

There may be something to this. I'd call her impudent. In class, she had no problem speaking out of turn. She was certainly bright, but I had never thought of her as extraordinarily intelligent.

Hannah recalls that after the war, she asked Mrs. Kuperus, the principal, whether she could show the school to her husband.

"When we were at the school with her, I asked, 'Did you see anything special in Anne at the time?' She said she hadn't, but I think she was right when she remarked 'When a girl at that age is removed from friends, plants, animals—from everything, really—and you put her in a home with only adults, everything develops much faster. Who knows—if there had been no war, she might not have become a great writer until she was thirty.' Circumstances sped up everything, including her development as a writer. She wrote so beautifully, especially for a girl that age."

"And she also spoke perfect Dutch, without any accent—while one of her friends, a certain Hanneli Goslar, still had a German accent," I say teasingly.

Hannah laughs. "We came from Berlin and spoke German at home. Not so at the Franks', where they had two Dutch-speaking daughters. My mother knew Dutch well, but my father didn't really. My mother was very good with languages, and with Greek and Latin, too, for that matter."

"My mother was born in the French-speaking part of Brussels," I say, "but during the First World War, she moved to the neutral Netherlands to be safer. That's where she met my father, *und von Spass kommt Ernst und der Ernst bin Ich* [it started as fun and turned into earnest, and I am this Ernest]. In her later years, she still had a Belgian accent."

I ask about Anne's supposed love of movies.

"I don't know," Hannah says, "but she certainly loved movie stars. They really weren't of any interest to me, so I never collected film-star photographs like the ones she had on her wall in the Secret Annex. *You Can't Take It with You* was a film that deeply affected me at the time—it had to do with wealthy people who couldn't take their money to the grave with them. Occasionally, my mother would take me to the Cineac movie house, where they showed children's films on a regular basis. I don't know whether or how frequently Anne used to go. We both loved Shirley Temple films."

My unusual interest in games may be a professional aberration, but it's to get a more complete picture of our youth that I ask about the games Hannah and Anne used to play—assuming they played any at all.

"Absolutely!" Hannah says enthusiastically. "Monopoly and Parcheesi. We were really crazy about Monopoly, which we played all the time."

Before we continue our conversation about the past, we play a game I've brought for Hannah; then we decide to take a walk through the city. Near a windmill, we encounter a field trip for one of the lower grades of a secondary school. The boys and girls are in peak condition. Each has almost too much energy for one person and is shouting, jumping up and down, and running around. It is all we can do not to be trampled by all that youthful exuberance.

Marvelous.

part 2

Going Underground

(Age Fourteen)

The phrase "going underground"—"onderduiken" in Dutch—was not a familiar one for us at first. We used to talk about "hiding" so we wouldn't have to "go to the camps." Like the rest of the population, we had no idea that these were *Vernichtungslager* (extermination facilities) since the Germans always referred to them as labor camps.

As time went on, all kinds of restrictions were imposed on Dutch Jews. Financially, they were having a very hard time, which explains the willingness of many to go to the so-called labor camps. They initially saw this as a way to avoid hunger and illness. There, at least, they thought they'd be fed. This ghastly delusion helped contribute to the killing of approximately 80 percent of the Jews in the Netherlands. The Green Police—the Germans responsible for maintaining order and other everyday duties—had the addresses of almost every Jew in Amsterdam eligible for the camps. When my parents and I discovered that we were about to be arrested, my parents asked a neighbor if I could stay at his house for a while. This neighbor was Jewish himself, and my parents made clear to him the seriousness of the situation. My sister had already been sent to Belgium.

I was at his house from about seven in the evening on. Everything seemed normal until we heard the Green Police, known to be as cold as they were merciless, enter our house next door. I felt my heart in my throat, and I flew underneath the neighbor's bed as fast as I could. From there, I could hear the Germans stomping around our house in search of us. I had no idea where my father and mother were at that moment and could only hope that they, too, had made a safe getaway. It was long after the Germans had left that I came out from under the bed. I must have been as white as a sheet, and for quite a while, I sat in the living room, numb with anxiety, until I was introduced to one of the neighbor's friends. There's not much I remember about the man except that he worked for Rademaker's Haagsche Hopjes, a candy manufacturer. It was an exhilarating discovery for a child.

Holding me by the shoulders, our neighbor asked, "Would you please take this boy in for a while?" The neighbor himself was probably not terribly keen on hiding a fellow Jew, or else he had realized that a hiding place right next door to my old house wasn't such a wise choice. I'll never know, but I wasn't there for more than three hours—three of the most suspenseful in my life. Finally, the candy maker and I walked over to his house on the IJselstraat—I don't recall the exact address—where I was temporarily put up. For a month, I hid in his home without seeing my parents or my sister. One day, a visitor arrived. To my utter surprise, I was introduced to him and when I told him my name was Maurice Coster, as it still was then, he said dryly, "Well, Maurice, you will call me Uncle Jan."

Accompanied by Uncle Jan, I took the train to Apeldoorn and continued by bus to Vaassen. There we visited the Reverend Van Deelen, whose manner quickly put me at ease. Dutch Reformed and the father of twelve children, he took his obligations seriously. After we had something to eat, he told Chris, his oldest son, to take me to a different address. We left on foot, heading east in the direction of the city of Deventer, to a farmhouse that bore the name *De*

Wulfte. (Built in 1771, it still stands there, the date stamped in large iron numbers on its facade.)

This is where the Zweers family lived. They had already been notified of my arrival.

IT WAS TO BE AN EXTRAORDINARY period for me, during which I did my best to ignore my anxieties about the future and the loss of an ordinary adolescence in which war and the fear of betrayal played no role. It wasn't terribly difficult for me to do so in this new environment, though, since as a boy who'd been raised in the big city, the countryside proved to be a wonderful distraction. There were cows, sheep, pigs, and a beautiful orchard—all utterly fascinating to a young boy from Amsterdam.

At the farm, especially early on, I was given food that was rich in fat and calories. Among other things, we used to eat *balkenbrij,* a culinary novelty for me, which consisted of flour and small bits of pork intestine. It was a hard mash, sliced and served cold. The farmer's wife, who was healthy and full-bodied herself, thought I was just a bag of bones. When I spread butter on my bread, she would add two more thick layers. It was ultimately too much fatty food for my body to handle: I was soon covered in boils.

I lived at this De Wulfte farmhouse for three months. Of course, as a Jew, I had to keep a low profile, and I missed my parents and Amsterdam, but life at the farm was so agreeable that there were times I'd momentarily forget all my misery.

I HAD TO LEAVE THE FARM once rumors began to spread about me. Somehow, local people had discovered that a young Jewish boy was hiding there. It's not entirely implausible that some jealousy was involved: for their efforts, the Zweers family received a small remuneration. I can't know whether that was the reason or whether the wrong people simply found out about me. In any event, I was in danger. Fortunately, I was moved from the farm in time.

Due to ever-increasing poverty, it wasn't unusual for Jews to be sold out to the Germans in exchange for money. In 1943, the deportations of Dutch Jews to the camps had begun to decline. In response, the Germans decided to offer financial incentives. Thirty, and then fifty, collaborators were hired and paid to hunt for Jews. Who were these people? Ordinary Dutchmen, frequently unemployed social outcasts, who in their greed were willing to turn over their Jewish countrymen. Purposeful and calculating, they traveled the country as if they were merely exercising a perfunctory civic duty, arresting men, women, and children as young as two or three. During the war, these men tracked down between eight and nine thousand victims, most of whom were sent to the concentration camps via the Netherlands Theater in Amsterdam and Camp Westerbork. Sometimes these Jews were not even arrested but murdered on the spot.

What was a human life worth? How much did a captured Jew bring in? Initially, about 7.50 guilders, which amounts to a bit more than thirty euros (about forty-five dollars) today.

Having heard rumors of these collaborators, it was absolutely necessary to be able to relocate at a moment's notice. My departure from De Wulfte wasn't a step backward—quite the contrary.

I moved in with a Mr. and Mrs. Van Beek, with whom I would stay until Liberation Day, which in my case would be April 17, 1945. The Van Beeks had no children of their own and seemed happy to receive a "ready-made" child—and an obedient one at that. I was fourteen years old and clearly seemed to be well-reared. Barend van Beek was the headmaster of the local Christian elementary school. I would become like a son to him and he like a father to me. In the winter, we'd go skating together. Once a week, I visited Reverend Van Deelen's son Chris to play chess. Chris was my age and, like me, wasn't a farmer's son.

I went to the same school as Chris did, for, unlike other children in hiding, I *was* able to go to school. It was all due to the fact that a few years earlier, after the German occupation, my father had failed to complete the required form concerning the origin of my grandparents. The Germans clearly had it in for the Jews, but in the Netherlands, many of us didn't realize it—especially at first. We didn't want to realize it. Hitler had been in power since 1933. The barbaric destruction of Jewish homes and stores in Berlin the infamous Kristallnacht—had taken place in 1938, and the expulsion of Jews from Germany had been an official reality since 1939. In spite of these early signs, many people completed those forms anyway.

Had the incomplete form been an act of resistance on my father's part? Or had he simply forgotten or procrastinated? Had it been laziness or fear? I'm afraid I'll never know. Either way, some civil servant laid eyes on the incomplete form and wrote down that I had two non-Jewish and two Jewish grandparents—in other words, not the four grandparents that I had in reality, with the result that I didn't have a *J* stamped on my identity card. For some inexplicable reason, this anonymous bureaucrat radically changed my life, and possibly even saved it.

My parents paid the Van Beeks about sixty-five guilders ($390) a month to hide me. I've no clue whether that was a reasonable or an unreasonable amount of money. I suspect that whether they were paid or not, they would have hidden anyone, no matter what, and that they would have treated any other child as their own, too.

In the early days of my time in Vaassen, my mother would visit the Van Deelen family once a month. That's how I knew she was alive, loved me, and under the circumstances was doing reasonably well. She didn't look Jewish, so she was able to move about with relative ease. Much later I found out that Mother had a false identity card, even with a name vaguely resembling her own.

I chose my new name after reading a book whose protagonist was named Theo. I rarely used the family name Van Beek and generally went by my own, Coster.

At the secondary school in Apeldoorn, the religious education was Christian. I myself knew absolutely nothing about Christianity. The New Testament was barely familiar to me, but fortunately, Barend gave me some help. He would read a chapter of the Bible before each hot meal—normally that was lunch—and so I learned something, at least. I'd grown up knowing very little about religion, despite having had my bar mitzvah at the beginning of the war.

At school, no one except the principal knew my true identity. That was very much to my advantage because the son of the leader of the local NSB—the Dutch Nazi party—was in my class.

I used to bike to school. There was a checkpoint along the way, where the police occasionally asked to see my ID, but—as it lacked the *J*—it always went quite smoothly. Whenever necessary, I'd tell them I was Mr. Van Beek's nephew.

NO MATTER HOW NICE Barend van Beek may have been, he seemed to confine his social life to his colleagues. Thus, he would sometimes visit with Mr. Akkerman, the principal of a Catholic elementary school, and Mr. Douma, the head of a middle school. On those occasions, I would go along with him to meet their children, which included two boys, Paul and Bo, and a girl, Ted. All three of them were roughly my own age. I'd spend time with them and so met other children as well. Sometimes the Van Beeks' nieces would spend time with us in Vaassen. I suspect that I owe my relatively normal adolescence to these friendships: they always teach you something.

Bo, Ted, and I would sometimes go swimming at a local farm. The farmer had dug out part of one of his pastures and turned it into an outdoor swimming pool, with a small flowing stream that continually freshened the water. Still young, I wasn't fully aware of the significance of being Jewish. But I knew that my circumcision, of course, had to be concealed at all times. For that reason, even a contest to see who could pee the farthest—and what boy hasn't participated in that?—was problematic for me. During my years underground, I couldn't be seen naked—not in front of the boys and certainly not in front of any girls! Swimming would have been a problem, too, were it not for the fact that the farmer had been good enough to add real changing stalls to his homemade swimming pool.

I once saw some boys playing with homemade toy airplanes. I tried to absorb as best I could what the planes looked like, but once I tried to build one back home, I realized I didn't know what materials they'd used. Instead of balsa wood, I used heavy oak and beech wood for the weight-bearing sections, and rather than oiled or varnished paper, I took cotton fabric to form the body. I proudly brought the result of many hours of sawing, gluing, and stretching to show the boys. They were polite enough to say they thought my airplane was very handsome but predicted that it wouldn't stay in the air very long. And they were right.

Generally speaking, the Germans didn't seek out regular contact with the Dutch population. I, for one, never had a casual chat with any of them and preferred taking the long way around when I saw any soldiers in German uniform. There was a military encampment in the Cannenburgh, a castle in Vaassen. I don't remember very much about any patrols, but I do know we had curfews.

In the late summer of 1944, shortly after the Allies had been defeated at the Dutch town of Arnhem, my mother came to live with the Van Beeks as well. Around the same time, the school next to our house was confiscated by a company of Dutch volunteers in the Waffen-SS. It soon became clear that we hadn't merely acquired a group of SS soldiers as neighbors but that some of them were also moving in with us.

Their commander, a lieutenant who'd been housed with us, looked perfectly normal; I wouldn't be able to recognize him today. He was a fairly unpleasant officer who made it absolutely clear that he looked down on us in every way. In his eyes, we were so obtuse that we didn't even know that "Deutschland über alles" ("Germany is superior") was true.

He was accompanied by another volunteer named Hendriks, a boot polisher. With his dark blond hair, he looked like a typical Dutchman. In contrast to his superior, he recognized that Germany was losing the war. I rather liked him despite his unsettling crafty manner. As it turned out later, he knew how to look out for himself.

As soon as these two moved in, I was forced to address my mother as "aunt." I didn't even think of it as a problem: I simply did it. I had to if I was to survive. Though it might seem hard to imagine for someone who's never been through a war, it was the norm for children like me to pretend to be someone else and play with friends who did the same. We were performing a kind of play—only it was real life and our lives depended upon it.

The Van Beeks' house had three bedrooms and a study. The lieutenant had the study and a small adjoining bedroom. Hendriks slept downstairs in the pantry. My mother slept in my former bedroom, while I stayed in the same room as Mr. and Mrs. Van Beek, whom I called father and mother.

From the moment I first came to Vaassen to the end of the war, I never once saw my father. He had gone underground in the small town of Hattem. He looked more Jewish than either my mother or me, and so for him, it was better never to be seen at all. He was forced to be "cellular" as we used to call it then: locked up inside his house.

It was Hendriks who took me along one day to the Apeldoorn Canal to go fishing with a hand grenade. It goes without saying that I was never totally at ease with him, but at the same time, I was also excited to spend some time with that somewhat sinister character. At home, they didn't make an issue of my being with him; after all, we didn't have any choice. It was wise to be on good terms with him, and besides, it made a difference for us that Hendriks was convinced the war was a lost cause for the Germans.

Nobody that I knew of had electricity or a radio at this time. Hendriks said, "If you get ahold of a radio, I'll take care of the electricity. Then we can listen to the BBC." As it turned out afterward, this was shortly before the Liberation.

The two men from the SS lived with us for three weeks. Then they moved on, and I thought they'd be gone from my life for good.

THERE WAS THE RESISTANCE, too, and I later realized I'd actually been in direct contact with some of its members during the war: the Reverend Van Deelen undoubtedly belonged to a local group of Resistance operatives. He may not have offered any armed resistance—he didn't place any bombs or set up any ambushes—but he did organize risky operations such as hiding Jews with farmers' families. Not that we were directly aware of this, but it seems highly unlikely that we were the only ones.

DURING THE WAR, I fared pretty well, and that may be the reason why, at the time, I never dwelled much on what an unusual—and for so many, a horrific—

period it must have been. But when you're in the middle of it all, you haven't the faintest idea how long it will go on, and especially as a child, you adapt quickly, no matter how much circumstances deviate from what you know as normal.

As the war progressed, the Germans' restrictions were imposed ever more harshly. There wasn't much else to do but live from one day to the next, with the somber awareness that things were unlikely to improve soon and could easily get worse—especially since news about how things were progressing was hard to come by. True, you'd occasionally hear part of a BBC broadcast, and sometimes you might even get ahold of a copy of the Allied newspaper *The Flying Dutchman.* The Allies disseminated the *Flying Dutchman* from the air. Sometimes, as I was riding my bike, I'd see where the pamphlets had landed and would go over to pick one up, not thinking for a second about the risk I was taking—the Germans didn't exactly encourage us to read Allied propaganda. As time went by, I had a pretty sizeable collection, which I donated to the Netherlands Institute for War Documentation after it was all over. Nonetheless, all in all, the news was sparse. Times were, and continued to be, uncertain.

In spite of the power wielded by the Nazis, I never believed that the Netherlands would actually become

German. As young as we were, we were absolutely convinced that the Germans were on the wrong track altogether. Apparently, they hadn't understood that as soon as America became involved, it would be all over for Germany. Today, we can see they simply had no clue about the Americans' ability to produce matériel. Indeed, it *was* unimaginable: arms and munitions factories such as Remington committed to manufacturing serious quantities of ammunition, and even Ford committed to using its factories to make tanks instead of cars. The Americans' commitment to the war effort was of incalculable importance.

Of course, for me, all of this is retrospective knowledge, but the Germans ought to have realized at the time the productive capacity on the other side of the Atlantic, at least in theory. Surely the Germans had spies in the United States.

They also underestimated the challengers of the eastern front, where they penetrated deeper and deeper into Russia, until they ran aground near Moscow. We had no inkling of what was happening there. The area where fighting took place was huge, and we weren't aware of the Russians' capabilities. We were hoping far too much for news of glorious Russian victories, which, unfortunately, we never received. However, they did have the advantage of being able to retreat as far as they wanted into their vast country, which forced the Germans to occupy an immense amount of land. It contributed to their ultimate defeat: even without any resistance to deal with, they simply didn't have enough soldiers to keep the region fully occupied. In the harsh and fatally exhausting winter of 1941, a continued attack was no longer an option for the Germans, and the distance was too great to retreat. Consequently, more than 830,000 German soldiers died in Russia over a period of nineteen months.

IN THE LARGER CITIES in the Netherlands, food shortages became a problem quite early on. Finding enough to eat each day was extremely difficult, especially for those in hiding. In the rural areas, though, it was easier. Many people knew a farmer or two who'd be willing to part with some food without causing any trouble.

As school principal, Mr. Van Beek was on good terms with the local farmers. I never had to endure true hunger because whenever we needed something, I'd hit the road, visiting farmers for some potatoes or the ingredients for black bread, which we ate all the time. We had our own rye flour ground in a mill, and if there was no flour, we'd eat rye porridge—healthy stuff, it's true, though it did get to be monotonous. We also ate plenty of the fruit that grew in the principal's orchard: cherries, gooseberries, plums, red and white currants, star apples, and pears. Finding fruit was no problem.

What *was* a real problem was bicycle tires. When all the spare ones were gone, I was forced to wrap a garden hose around my rims and ride on that, though it turned out to work fairly well. It was a little more awkward, but flat tires were no longer an issue thanks to the thickness of the hose. Besides, I didn't exactly travel far—ten kilometers (about six miles) at most.

In Amsterdam, on the other hand, bicycles were confiscated. Initially, only those that belonged to Jews had to be turned in, but later it became mandatory for everyone. In general, life was harder in the big cities, where the Nazi oppression was far more present. Bombings were much more common and, contrary to popular belief, came from the Allies, not the Germans. The latter didn't bomb the Netherlands, at least not after Rotterdam was bombed on May 14, 1940, destroying the entire heart of the city.

I thank my lucky stars that I myself never had to witness a similar attack. As far as I knew, the iron works of Vaassen, which could easily have been a strategic target, were never attacked. Occasionally, a downed plane would fall from the air. From our house, dogfights were visible to the naked eye—we could watch a Messerschmidt and a Spitfire attacking each other, for example.

Only once did I go and look at a plane that had crashed. It was an Allied bomber, probably a B–24 Liberator, that had come down in a pasture. There were no people inside: apparently they'd already escaped. The plane hadn't burned, so it must have been an emergency landing. It was a lonely wreck that lay there. What could I do? I rummaged around a little, but there wasn't much that seemed to be of any value. In the end, I took a string of machine gun bullets with me. They hadn't been fired. Once home, I had no idea what to do with them, so I took them to the school—the layout of which I knew like the back of my hand—and hid them in a hollow space between two walls.

Every now and then, the German soldiers would take a look inside the school building, but they never did discover the string of bullets.

Prisoners for Exchange

In Hannah's sunlit apartment in Jerusalem, I talk about my wartime experiences: hiding out, the Van Beek family, and life in the country.

"I have to say that it was not at all bad—almost pleasant, in fact." Feeling a bit timid, I ask, "And what about you? What was your experience like?"

"Unpleasant," Hannah says, laughing.

I ask whether she'd been hidden for any period of time. It seems logical to me that just about everyone who was at risk of deportation must have considered going underground or else actually did, if only for a few days.

"No, never," she answers. I remark that she had just let herself be arrested, then, and she looks at the floor uncomfortably. The phrase sounds a little blunt in Dutch, I realize. But since Hannah and I have been living in Israel for decades now and our conversation is taking place in three languages—Hebrew, Dutch, and a stray German sentence here and there; we don't let it bother us.

She says, "I have a little sister—who's still alive, thank God—twelve years younger than I, born in October 1940. My mother always wanted a large family and became pregnant with her third child in 1942."

Hannah believes that it was common for the Germans to make an exception for pregnant women when deportations were happening and so allowed her to stay home with her family.

"Nice of them, right? It may have saved us in 1942. We stayed in our house on the Zuider Amstellaan, for you don't take a pregnant woman into hiding, although some people did. In our case, it was a very good thing that my mother didn't because everything went wrong. Both my mother and the baby died during childbirth. We had a Jewish obstetrician and yet on October 27 it all went wrong. It was a little boy."

In addition to the pregnancy, Hannah's family may have had something more decisive to fall back on. In the Netherlands in 1942, if you wanted to stay at home, you needed what they called a *Sperr.* It was a stamp that exempted you from deportation—for the time being, at least. The stamp was primarily given to Jews who could be useful to the Germans: women who could sew uniforms for the soldiers, for example. Even if they received a *Sperr,* they couldn't take it for granted. Nothing was ever certain.

"My father couldn't sew uniforms and yet we were given the stamp or else I wouldn't be sitting here now," Hannah says. "We received a *Sperr* for two reasons. First, because we had a Paraguayan passport. This is how that came about: we were Jews who'd fled Germany. We came to Holland via England. Because my father couldn't work on the Sabbath, they had no use for him in England, even though he'd been offered a good job that paid well. Once in the Netherlands, they didn't extend his passport. But the fact was that my father had been junior minister of domestic affairs and press secretary of the Prussian cabinet in Berlin. So then they gave us an official document designating us as 'stateless.' Fortunately, an uncle in Switzerland was able to purchase passports for us at a South American consulate, and that's how we acquired a Paraguayan passport. The Germans knew perfectly well that we had nothing to do with Paraguay, but they were intent on keeping a small group of Jews in reserve, about four thousand, to be exchanged some day for German prisoners of war of the British.

"The second reason we received that stamp was connected to a similar plan: in Switzerland, negotiations were taking place between Germany and England, where an agreement was reached on the so-called 'Palestine certificates.' These were exclusively for people who had parents, children, and siblings in Palestine and because of the war could no longer leave Holland to go anywhere else. The certificate allowed you to leave and settle in Palestine. The Germans conferred such certificates in exchange for the return of a given number of Germans from Palestine. My father applied for that certificate as well. Granted, we had no ties with Palestine, but my father had been not only one of the two most highly placed Jewish civil servants in the German government—until Hitler came to power, of course—but was also a leader in the Jewish community. He toured Germany regularly to give lectures on Palestine. In addition, he was prominent within the newspaper world and, in that capacity, was able to write about Palestine as much as he wanted, both for German and Jewish papers."

"Had he ever been there?" I ask.

"No, never. My grandfather had. He did the same thing as my father, also lecturing and so on. He was a renowned criminal lawyer."

The documents, stamps, and other ploys worked until June 20, 1943. That day, a massive roundup took place in Amsterdam South, at the crack of dawn. Hannah, her father, and her sister were transported to Westerbork. Her father would not survive the camp.

There's so much more that I want to ask Hannah, but our time is up, and I have to leave. Hannah is the only one to have spoken with Anne in Bergen-Belsen, and I can only hope we'll have time to talk about that later on.

WE SAY GOOD-BYE in the scorching heat of the Israeli sun. Eyal and I barely speak on the ride back; my head is reeling with the memories of school and of my youth in Amsterdam. Slowly, I begin to realize what I've gotten myself into with this project. Not only am I myself revisiting that dreadfully dark time in history, but I'm also asking several people with whom I haven't spoken in years to do the same.

Nanette's Clock

A few weeks later, I'm flying from Tel Aviv to the Netherlands. Because I don't have a home in Amsterdam, nor do I want to saddle my sister or my acquaintances in Buitenveldert with my unexpected visit, I take a room at the Amstel Hotel.

It had seemed like a good idea to Ora and me to get the former students together for a group conversation. Later in the week, we could then take short trips to places that were relevant not only for Anne Frank but for us as well—Eyal considers specific locations to be crucial to our film. Obviously, there is the Secret Annex, but I also want to go to the lyceum. Perhaps we can go to Westerbork. Whoever is interested is welcome to come with us. No matter what, it will be a week filled with memorable reunions.

While I'm enjoying the luxury of the elegant Amstel Hotel, Nanette Blitz Konig has opted for the Hilton, her favorite hotel in Amsterdam. When I had told her about my plans, she said to my great surprise that it was important to her to be there, too, and so she has left São Paulo to join us in Amsterdam.

Nanette and I have agreed to meet on a small street in Amsterdam South. In her youth, it was *the* upper-class section of town, as it still is today.

The reunion with Nanette is remarkable. I know what she looks like because we've spoken frequently via videophone, but I'm still surprised to see how full of vitality she really is and how much younger than her actual age she looks: slender, silver-haired, and stylishly dressed in a perfectly tailored outfit of handsome fabric. (She tells me afterwards that she has everything custom made according to her own design.)

We're standing behind the house where her family lived when the war broke out. Nanette tells me that her parents had three children. A nurse had lived with them because Nanette's youngest brother, born in 1932, had heart trouble, and she left when the boy died in 1936. They called him a "blue baby"; his heart valves didn't close properly, and he couldn't get enough oxygen. Nanette's mother was told right after he was born that he would die young, but she did everything in her power to make his life tolerable. He died in November 1936, at just four years of age.

Nanette's other brother was two years older than she. "He was deported, and although I tried everything I could to find out, I don't really know how he met his end. Either he was shot or gassed, or killed some other way."

I ask about her childhood in general. How was it growing up in this part of Amsterdam?

She tells me that as a child, she did indeed feel privileged. The Blitz family would travel to Switzerland and England frequently, which was quite unusual at the time.

"I suppose my youth here was quite happy, except for 1936, when my mother was as brave as she was sad. We had an antique English clock at home and my mother walked me over to it. 'This clock only moves forward, never goes back again,' she said. For someone who'd just lost a child on the floor above that was a courageous thing to say to her daughter. I don't know to what extent she actually felt it at that moment, but the fact is that she expressed it. Words that gave me a great deal of strength later on."

The clock survived the war, and Nanette still has it today.

"I was seven when my youngest brother died. They came to pick my older brother and me up from school. I've never seen my mother hysterical, not even on that day. She was serious, calm, and knew exactly what she wanted to tell me. 'If you'd like to go upstairs,' she said to my older brother, 'to see your little brother, then you should.' Whether he did or not, I don't remember now.

"Because of his illness, I'd never played much with my little brother, so I didn't miss him as a playmate. I was probably too young to realize what it all meant. I did understand that this was a serious matter. Just imagine the interior of a Jewish home where someone has just died: every framed photograph is placed face down, and every mirror is covered. It made a deep impression on me. And to see my mother like that was horrible. Subsequently, both she and I were very sick.

"In those days, women didn't go to funerals, so I didn't either. My mother's outlook was that life simply continues, and that's precisely what happened. We were in mourning for six months. Then my father said, 'Look, we've shown our respect and our sorrow, but we have two other children. Let's take off these black clothes and go on with our life.'

"And my mother did. Better yet, she decided to learn how to ride a bike, something she'd always been afraid to do. She never had time before because of the baby's illness.

"My father was a studious man, constantly upstairs. We were always allowed to read anything. When we didn't understand something, we'd ask him for an explanation first, before we'd put the book aside.

"I suppose I was raised in a very liberal way—nothing was taboo at home. It was very inspiring to me."

"Did Anne ever visit you here?" I ask.

"I can't recall that she ever dropped in," Nanette says. "Right after we switched to the Jewish lyceum, we still owned bikes and could take the tram. But it wasn't long before that changed: from June 1942 on, all means of transportation were forbidden to us Jews. Because of the roundups, we'd walk home in groups, and we weren't in the same group because Anne lived on Merwedeplein while I was in Amsterdam's Old South section. I did go to her birthday party in June, right before she went into hiding. In class, we sat very near each other.

"We were totally different. Anne was very vivacious. She always wanted to be the center of attention—she loved that. I don't think I wanted to pay that much attention to her. I was different physically, too. I was more solidly built; she was more petite than me. I truly believed she was a perfectly normal girl, just like every other girl. It was absolutely unimaginable that she'd become so famous."

I'm quite curious whether Nanette remembers that I was at that birthday party as well, but just to be sure, I ask her more generally what she remembers about me.

"I don't remember that much about you. We had little cliques, and I know you were in my class, but at that age, I wasn't interested in boys at all. I vaguely remember what you looked like; you had curly hair, I think.

"I remember Albert better. Jacqueline van Maarsen—she was a very good friend of Anne's, maybe her best friend, and she was a good friend of mine, too. But because Anne tended to be rather jealous, she wasn't supposed to know that." Nanette smiles. "I don't know if Anne ever discovered it. After Anne went into hiding, Jacqueline confessed that she'd kept silent about our friendship. When I was picked up about a year later, in September 1943, Jacqueline had lost both Anne and me."

Arrested

We walk over to the Van Baerlestraat to see the front of Nanette's family home. She lived here for thirteen years. The facade is hidden behind scaffolding. The traffic is noisy, but Nanette laughs when I ask whether all that street noise used to bother her.

"You sleep through everything when you're a child. My older brother developed an intense interest in public transportation and in trams in particular. He began to keep track of the arrival times of the trams.

Not only those that had a stop near our house, but the other stops as well."

The Rijksmuseum and Stedelijk Museum are behind us. Nanette tells me how her mother, who kept an eye on the exhibitions that were shown there, used to take her children to the museum—a real privilege, she now remarks.

The ground floor of the house was used as a bank. "The Bank of Amsterdam," Nanette says. "During the bombings early in the war, this floor served as an air-raid shelter. If I remember correctly, we had to go into the vaults whenever we were in danger."

Amsterdam was spared in the end, but Rotterdam's historic center was destroyed on May 14, 1940, between 1:30 and 1:45 in the afternoon by ninety-seven thousand kilos (over two hundred thousand pounds) of German antipersonnel bombs. It was to be Utrecht's turn the following day, until the Netherlands surrendered to Germany.

"My father worked as a manager at the Bank of Amsterdam, at its headquarters on the Heerengracht. When Jewish employees had to be fired during the war, he was not at risk at first because of the important position he held, but shortly thereafter, he was forced to resign 'for the sake of the business.' It was very hard on him; he'd been working there since 1914. Once he was out of work, he aged rapidly; he turned gray. He looked drained, and he kept losing weight until he was almost skeletal. The dismissal hit him hard, and he blamed himself. He was fairly well-known internationally, but he never thought the situation would get so out of hand, so he never tried to get us out of the Netherlands. I never held him responsible, because I didn't know what he was going through at the time." Nanette says that her father was taking care not only of his own family but also of his parents and his mother-in-law.

"He always used to say that even before the war, there was latent anti-Semitism. 'Despite the fact that I'm a Jew, I'm still a bank director,' he once told me. But then, the bank obviously had Jewish money."

Nanette had not personally experienced any anti-Semitism before this. "At least not that I can recall. But, of course, I was well aware of a general anti-Jewish atmosphere. From the moment the war broke out and Europe was struggling with a great deal of unemployment, the voices claiming that Jews had too much power grew louder and louder. And as they were persecuted, anti-Semitism became an undeniable fact.

"As I said, my father never tried to get us across the border before the war. Like many Jews in the Netherlands, he may have been a bit naive. He assumed that the country would remain neutral as it had been during the First World War, even though the news of the German regime's anti-Jewish laws certainly reached the Netherlands. But the Jews thought that such a thing could never happen here, and by the time they recognized their mistake, it was too late. As you know, the great majority of the Dutch Jews did not survive the war."

In the meantime, we've been looking at the house from the sidewalk for quite a while now. In and of itself, it doesn't look very different from the other houses on the block. I ask Nanette if she has any particular feelings or specific memories as she gazes at its facade.

She takes a deep breath. "Well, what should I say? We used to have a lot of visitors, from abroad as well. I learned a great deal in this house, read a lot. I have many good memories and also many bad ones. One of the worst is of the day that the Germans came: there was banging on the door, shouting, and we had to leave immediately. I can still hear the door slamming shut behind me. Although I knew it might well happen, at that moment it was an incredible shock. I was leaving an entire life behind in exchange for an uncertain future. We traveled to Westerbork from the train station."

Nanette looks around and recalls that they went to the station by tram, not by truck, as was more common during roundups.

"We were picked up early in the morning. I was fourteen and still in bed. They shouted, 'Raus, raus! Schnell!' [Outside, outside! Quick!] as they pounded on the door with their rifle butts. We knew exactly what was going on. It was the German police, not the Dutch, although they were frequently involved in these kinds of raids, too. They had our full names on a list, and they made it very clear that we had to come with them.

"I had a backpack with clothes, sweaters, a pair of boots, and a coat. Because we were lucky enough to be on that Palestine list thanks to my father's work, we were never branded or shaven, and our clothes weren't taken from us."

I ask her if there was any violence when they were arrested.

"No," Nanette answers. "Not then, not later either."

We take another look at the door through which the family was taken from their home. I ask her what her brother's reaction was at that moment.

"He was sixteen. He didn't say a word. I'm sure he was traumatized. Other than those Germans with their rifles cocked in hand, there was no one around. None of us spoke. Later, it turned out that we were one of the last families to be hauled off. In September 1943, the Germans considered the Netherlands to be 'free of Jews.'"

Nanette speculates whether the Dutch population could have done more to help the Jews. The percentage of Dutch people involved in the Resistance was relatively small, she observes, and no matter how laudable it was that there was some opposition to the Germans, it's impossible to determine how effective it actually was. It is still hard for her to remember that each train that left for Westerbork was always empty when it returned. "And each train that went from Westerbork to Sobibor always came back empty, too."

Looking back, she wonders if perhaps too many Dutch people remained passive.

"Do you think it would be any different today?" I ask as cyclists zoom past us. "Would today's generation be substantially different?"

"No, I guess not. The people of Amsterdam today wouldn't do anything different from what they did then. They'd be afraid to end up in the same train. Truth be told, the population did go on strike in February 1941 because of the restrictions imposed on the Jews. A strike that, of course, was very violently crushed, which upset the Jews immensely—from that moment on they became really anxious."

I tell Nanette that the February strike was astounding to the Jews I knew, to family as well as friends. Perfectly ordinary Amsterdam citizens—postal workers, railway and tram crews, dock workers—all went on strike over what was happening to us. We couldn't ever have imagined such a thing was possible, and we were overwhelmed by the protests.

I ask if she feels any anger here, at the front door on the Van Baerlestraat. Nanette's face tightens, and she gives me a serious look. "I try to remember all that's good and beautiful. Anger doesn't solve anything. We can only solve problems by looking at things head-on and realizing what exactly went wrong. We have to stay vigilant."

My documentary ought not to be anything more than a personal hobby, the time-consuming but harmless undertaking of an elderly man. Unfortunately, Nanette is more than right when she says that we must remain vigilant. It's essential that we continue to remember this history if we don't want to find ourselves in another period when concealment and deportations are the order of the day. I realize that this film is increasingly taking on the character of a mission for me.

Reunion at Merwedeplein

Three days later, the moment has arrived: all the classmates I was able to enlist are coming together today. We are to meet on the Merwedeplein. I take a taxi from the Amstel Hotel to the section of the city where all the streets are named for rivers, and I notice the weather is with us today: it's nice and warm, and the sun is shining, so there'll be no problem settling down outside on the grass. This isn't just about me but about everyone's personal histories, and I'm honored to see those who have come: Nanette Blitz Konig, Jacqueline Sanders van Maarsen, Lenie Duyzend, and Albert Gomes de Mesquita. Nanette has come from far-off Brazil and Albert from Eindhoven, while Jacqueline and Lenie both live in Amsterdam. Unfortunately, Hannah was unable to come from Israel. Thanks to Nanette, I've already found out some odds and ends about our former classmates ahead of time. After a successful career as a bookbinder, Jacqueline became a writer; as a girl, Lenie had gone into hiding in the forest; Albert became an engineer in Eindhoven. I'm very eager to learn more about them—what they thought about the school, whether and where they'd been in hiding, how they remember Anne—so I'm glad I'll also be seeing each of them separately later on.

Jacqueline's books deal with her experiences during the war, her family, and her friendship with Anne Frank, who in her famous diary mentions her as "Jopie." In addition, Jacqueline has quite an extraordinary personal history, as she will tell us in time. Her books made a deep impression on me and proved there always was a fine writer inside her waiting to come out. I worried I might feel nervous in Jacqueline's presence, but luckily, she is just as deeply engaged in the conversation as the rest of the group. No room for any nerves.

We're sitting on folding chairs in a circle on the grass. The Merwedeplein's rows of houses surround us. The Frank family used to live in one of them. Someone's placed a flower garland around the neck of the nearby bronze statue of Anne, which makes her look a little like a Hawaiian dancer, especially in this lovely weather. Here, beyond the city's busy center, it's wonderfully calm. People are talking of the old days, of children and grandchildren.

To open the discussion, I've brought an enlargement of an old class picture—not of our class at the lyceum but of our class at our old elementary school in 1937. I've had the photo for years, and there's no doubt this is the time to find out who's who. Perhaps my former classmates will recognize some children who were in the class. After all, we all lived in the same city. I only recognize myself and Mrs. de Haan, our teacher.

Lenie is the first to take a look at the picture. She removes her glasses and stares at it intently.

"Let's start by trying to find you." Albert tells us how he ran into a kindergarten classmate when he was thirty, who told him that "he'd not changed at all." "Apparently I still looked like a toddler," he grumbles, smiling.

Everyone laughs. Now I can actually remember him a little. Albert is simply still Albert, with the same scrutinizing and intelligent look in his eyes, while his features have visibly weathered over time.

I show Lenie which one I am. "How odd," she says. "I wouldn't have recognized you, although in my mind's eye, I have a very clear picture of you when we were in class together. You sat somewhere in the center row. Nanny and I sat close to the door."

My memory isn't as clear. I wonder if I would have recognized Lenie had I not known which one she was. Now that I know, I can see it—but that's always the case, of course. Her wavy black hair could have been a clue, and her glasses, too. But then, how many women with black hair and glasses have I run into during my life?

Albert has brought an old portrait of himself and shows it to us. Lenie comments that her memory of him is very different, too. "So there you are: your memory changes things, doesn't it? Especially after such a long time."

Jacqueline has brought something as well—something very special: her old poetry album.* "We are here now with only a part of our class," she says, "but those who are missing are also in here. That's what I wanted to show you. In her diary, Anne mentioned all the girls in her class, including Ilse Wagner, and—"

"I hope I'm not hurting anyone's feelings here, but that's the one I had a crush on," Albert interrupts. We laugh. "It meant nothing, of course. At that age . . ."

"Yes, she was very sweet," Jacqueline agrees. "I was very fond of her, too."

Out loud, she reads what Ilse wrote in the album. "She talks about 'a long and happy life,' but less than a year later, on April 2, 1943, she was killed in Sobibor. Just think how innocent we used to be. We knew nothing. And our parents didn't tell us very much either.

"Here are a few words that Hennie Metz wrote to me in July 1942. A year later, she was in Sobibor, too, just like Ilse, and probably gassed immediately.

---

* The poetry album is a traditional Dutch custom, popular with young girls, in which friends inscribe new or existing poems in the owner's book, often adding illustrations or stickers.—Trans.

Of all the ones who wrote in here, Anne Frank probably lasted the longest."

Jacqueline flips to the page where Anne left her message. "She wrote this in March 1942, and she died in Bergen-Belsen in March 1945." Jacqueline browses until she finds the page she's been looking for. "Betty Bloemendaal wrote this in April 1942 and was also killed in Sobibor on July 23, 1943."

"These notes seem innocent because in the summer of 1942, no Jewish children had been deported yet," Lenie remarks. "No children had disappeared yet. But then a year later, they suddenly stopped coming to school."

I ask Jacqueline if we may hear Anne's poem. Jacqueline reads aloud: "It was written in Amsterdam, March 23, 1942. Dear Jacque, always be a ray of sun / in school a good kid / dearest friend / and you'll be loved by everyone. In memory of your good friend, Anne Frank."

Going Underground

The conversation turns to going underground. Who went, when, and why? Lenie says that she went into hiding in late May 1943. She only attended the lyceum for the first year, then went to the Jewish Montessori Lyceum for a short while. Around that time, they met

Jews who'd fled Germany. "The German Jews had experienced much more than the Dutch Jews. They'd already been through so much in their own country," she says.

I think of Hannah and of Anne, who explained in her diary that her father had brought the family to the Netherlands in 1933 because they were "full-blooded" Jews. It was as early as that that the lives of German Jews were made miserable. In 1938, after Kristallnacht, many of their relatives escaped to North America.

When I tell them that my identity papers had no *J* because I seemed to have only two Jewish grandparents, Albert asks why I'd gone into hiding at all.

"It happened because my parents weren't going to come home again. Their papers did have a *J* and they were in danger, so they decided to go underground. What else could they do with me? Let me live by myself in the house? That was impossible, so they handed me off."

Jacqueline says that she actually did have two non-Jewish grandparents. "But since we were registered with the Jewish community, they considered us to be Jews. That's how I came to attend the lyceum as well. Halfway through the war, my mother took action and went to the Euterpestraat." That's the street—

today known as the Gerrit van der Veenstraat—where the offices of the SD, the German Secret Service, were located.

"My mother was Catholic, not Jewish. She was the kind of woman who would get anything done that she wanted done. Of course, it was also terrifying for her to confront a high-ranking officer, but she bamboozled him and let her charm do its work. Then there were papers that had to be retrieved from the south of France, which was a rather convoluted affair, but in the end, it all worked out. Halfway through the war, I was suddenly no longer Jewish," Jacqueline says.

"That's why you're here now, alive and well," I say.

"That's right. Otherwise, I certainly wouldn't have been here at all." She's silent for a moment until she remembers that she's still holding the poetry album. She glances at Lenie. "Lenie, would you like to read your poem again? Something you haven't seen in all these years."

Lenie looks up, surprised. "Sure. Of course." She carefully takes the old notebook and studies the page that Jacqueline opens for her, then reads: "April 21, 1942, Amsterdam-South. Dear Jacqueline, a happy laugh each day / a friendly word for all the way / enjoy your youth, enjoy your life / and always bring delight, not strife. Your classmate, Lenie Duyzend." She smiles and says that she never used to copy her poems but always wrote them herself.

Albert and I observe that boys didn't write in poetry albums at that time.

"Would you like to read your poem as well?" Jacqueline asks Nanette.

"Yes, of course. How wonderful you've still got all this. What a lovely memento."

"I wasn't in hiding. That makes all the difference."

Nanette begins: "March 19, 1942. Dear Jacqie. A good fairy lives on earth here / creating a thousand miracles dear / she's greatly loved and gets respect / from everyone she's ever met / That fairy skillfully does much good / and in every girl's heart should / live, for gentleness is her name. Your friend, Nanny Blitz. And then on the other side I wrote, Roses are red / Violets are blue / Sugar is sweet / And so, dear Jacky, are you."

We laugh.

Since Hannah isn't with us, Albert reads us her poem: "March 8, 1942. Dear Jacque, always be cheerful and merry / let your face show fun / and into every house you'll bring / joy and rays of sun. Your friend, Elisabeth Goslar. With a small portrait of her—that was quite unusual then, putting a photograph in a poetry album."

The conversation moves on to Anne's birthday party, which took place in the house right next to us.

"Were you there, too, Albert? Do you remember that movie, *Rin Tin Tin?*" I ask.

"Yes, I was there," he answers, "but I remember absolutely nothing about any *Rin Tin Tin.* I do remember some other film about jam-making. Otto Frank used to show that at parties. We were in one room and then there was an adjoining room that was all dark, with the screen. Otto Frank was in the pectin trade, but that was something I didn't know at the time. I thought it was terribly boring; it didn't interest me in the least."

"Miep Gies once told me that it was a publicity film for Opekta," Jacqueline says.

"I don't really remember that *Rin Tin Tin* film very well either," Nanette says. "What I do remember is that checkered album, her first diary. I can see it right now, lying on the table together with Anne's other presents," she says.

"I think she showed it to us. It wasn't on the table," Jacqueline says. "What I remember is that she was always very secretive about it. She'd received it the day before, and I'm sure she didn't leave it lying around on the table for a whole day."

"Be that as it may," Nanette says, "I did see it then and really noticed it. I had a diary myself, as everyone did at the time, but what I really loved was that checkered pattern. At home, we always used to say that the walls had ears, so you couldn't discuss anything, but somehow you really had to vent. That's why we wrote so much."

Jacqueline mentions that she didn't write, the sound of disappointment in her voice.

Anne Frank's Admirers

Get a group of men and women together, and soon the topic turns to love. In our case, we aren't concerned so much about who was going with whom, but rather who had his eye on Anne—and whether in our opinion, Anne was a pretty girl or not.

"I'm absolutely sure that the word *sexy* simply didn't exist for us in those days," I say. "The one thing I knew, and I was very aware of it, was that Anne was an attractive girl. But whether she knew that herself . . .

"In one of her diary entries, she writes, '*Do you remember?* How Maurice Coster was planning to present himself to Pim to ask his permission to see his daughter.' Maybe Anne thought I wanted to go steady with her."

"Was that true?" Jacqueline asks.

"I think it wasn't any more than some rumor she heard." I mention that we did bike to school together sometimes—not exactly a shocking story.

In her diary, Anne refers to me as "one of her many admirers." I honestly have no idea how she came up with that. And I can't quite account for what she writes about me later either.

From a blank cardboard notebook with a red-and-white checkered cover, Anne's diary turned into an international bestseller of monumental significance. If the Germans had taken the notebook with them after her capture, the *Diary* would never have been published.

After hearing a radio broadcast of a speech given by Gerrit Bolkenstein, the exiled minister of education, Anne had decided to make a copy of her notebook. Bolkenstein had called for testimonies such as diaries to be collected and published after the war, and Anne wanted to eventually use her diary as the basis for a book. In the process of copying, she omitted some passages she considered unimportant and added others with new thoughts.

Miep Gies was one of the women who'd helped the Franks during their period in hiding. After they were arrested, she saved the original diary and the copy. Without having read them, she returned them along with Anne's other papers to Otto after the war. He put together an abbreviated third edition, compiled from the original diary and its copy. The Dutch newspaper *Het Parool* gave it a very positive review even before it came out. Soon thereafter, it was placed with a publisher, and from that moment on, *The Diary of a Young Girl* has never been out of print in the Netherlands.

Foreign translations soon followed, although the international sales of Anne's book didn't really take off until a play based on the diary was produced in America. The back cover of my most recent copy of *The Diary* states that it has been published in more than thirty countries, with more than sixteen million copies sold.

She mentions me on page 12: "Maurice Coster is one of my many admirers, but he's a rather boring kid."

"WHAT I KNOW ABOUT ANNE," Jacqueline says, "is that she's described herself so well in her diary that we almost don't need to say anything else about her. Every now and then, she writes that she's very much the center of attention, but I don't really remember that. I don't think there were actually as many boys after her as she claims in her diary. Other than that, I think she's described her own personality very well. Honest and extraordinary, especially the way she writes about herself during the hiding period."

"I don't remember all that much about her," Albert says. "I was much too timid, and Anne was a full-fledged teenager at the time. So if you're talking about 'having a crush,' I was more liable to have one on the less dramatic types like Ilse Wagner. She was much more low-key."

"Anne was always chiding me for fiddling with my hair and my buttons," Nanette says. "And as I remember, she did always want to be the center of attention. She liked that. When I saw her in the camp later on, things were very different, of course."

"What's this?" I ask. "You saw her there?" I had known that Nanette had been in Bergen-Belsen, the same concentration camp to which Anne and her sister Margot had been deported, but this is something that she hadn't yet told me.

"Saw her and hugged her. Bergen-Belsen was a camp divided into several sections. I was in a different section from Anne. I'd first seen her through the barbed wire. She looked so awful that it took some time before I recognized her. The last time we'd seen each other was in July 1942, just before she went into hiding with her family. The shock of seeing her under these circumstances, in such a terrible state, was indescribable.

"At some point the barbed wire was removed. I assumed that Anne would still be on the other side in her section, and I went looking for her. And found her. From then on, I went to see her fairly often.

"We looked like skeletons, but Anne was convinced she'd survive the camps. She told me she'd continued writing in her diary while she was in hiding. She didn't want to publish it but wanted to use it as the basis for a book.

"Anne arrived in Bergen-Belsen in November, completely weakened. She told me about her experiences in Auschwitz. She didn't know what had become of her mother, who'd stayed behind in Poland.

"Later on, a girl arrived in my barracks and was assigned to the bed next to mine. She now lives in Haifa, Israel. We started talking, and she told me that Anne's mother had survived the selection. I passed it on to Anne, and the news renewed her courage. I also saw Margot. She died shortly before Anne. But it wasn't until after the war that I heard Hannah had also been in Bergen-Belsen. That's how split up that camp was."

In and Out of School

Every now and then, our discussion is interrupted by a small group of children passing by, catching our attention as they go to the nearby playground. They look to be about eight years old—four, five years younger than we were when we attended the lyceum with Anne. We've not finished talking about her quite yet, and I'll get to know her a little better over the course of the day.

Albert recalls that at the lyceum, he had Mrs. Biegel for biology. "She told us that when you put a horse and a donkey in the stable together, you'll end up with a mule. And I didn't understand how that worked. Anne Frank was quite prepared to explain it to me, but I wasn't really so keen on that—to the great amusement of the class, of course."

We laugh.

Nanette says, "We really were still quite naive then—very different from the youth of today."

It makes me smile to think of Anne, quite happy to provide Albert with some sex education in front of the whole class.

"Well, what I also remember of that summer of 1942," Albert says, "is that we were approaching summer vacation, and one of the teachers arranged to set up a class library. We could each bring in a book and then borrow from each other. I remember being criticized—I don't recall by whom—because my books were so childish. That may well have been true because I was a full year younger than the rest. I was good in math and not bad in language, but there were certain things I just wasn't ready for."

"I remember a few things about that library, too," Jacqueline says, "like the book I brought, my most beautiful one, of course. *Schoolidylle* was the title, first edition. It taught me a good lesson because the book disappeared in no time at all."

I wonder out loud whether there were any really good students at our school.

"We were all good students," Jacqueline says. "Otherwise, we wouldn't have attended the lyceum."

"The brightest one is in your poetry album, too," Albert remarks. "Betty Bloemendaal—she had the best report card in the class."

"Oh, that's very sad to think about, too," Jacqueline says. "Such a smart girl. Very quiet and very sweet." She looks at the note she's added to Betty Bloemendaal's page in the poetry album. "July 1943. I suppose that's the month in which she was gassed in Sobibor. Sometimes I research those things, and when the date matches that of her parents, you know exactly what happened. I checked up on my own nieces as well, and their dates also corresponded to those of their parents."

"What I really regret," says Nanette, "is that we don't have a group photograph of the class. What I do happen to have is a school picture that by a stroke of luck survived the war. When the Germans looted our house, they accidentally knocked one folder to the floor, which the neighbors found and saved. It contained my original school picture, like the one of Anne Frank." Nanette tells us that she donated her old picture to the Jewish Historical Museum where it still hangs. Her husband says occasionally that he's now married to a museum piece.

WE TRY TO REMEMBER what we used to do to amuse ourselves outside of school. Playing outdoors soon became difficult because everything was taboo for us quite early on. Bicycles had to be handed in at the end of our first year of school. Jacqueline tells us that Anne's bike had been stolen a week earlier, which she then reported to the police. "And it just so happens that about ten years ago, that report was found in the police records. Well, yeah, as soon as Anne Frank's name appears somewhere, it all becomes very interesting. In any event, once the bikes were gone, we'd walk to school."

Lenie says, "Yes, all those laws were enacted from the spring of 1941 on. We weren't allowed in the parks, we couldn't play any sports, we couldn't even sit in our own yard anymore."

"No, I wasn't allowed to be a boy scout any longer either," I add. "And I was really sorry about that because I loved being a scout."

"After all the laws were enforced, some people established a scout troop for Jewish children," Albert remembers. "I belonged to it for about a year, until that also was forbidden. At our final meeting, the scoutmaster gave a speech that made an enormous impression on me. He said, 'Right now we're on the blacklist. We're being reviled, mocked, and scorned from all sides. But remember this: Judaism has also created a great many beautiful things of which we can be proud.' When the war was over, I went in search of those beautiful things. I began to study modern Hebrew and became involved in the Jewish community. They even awarded me with a ribbon for these efforts."

Every one of us feels that because of the war, we missed part of our youth. Nanette remarks that she never had an adolescence. "We went straight from childhood to adulthood, by force of circumstance." She feels like she was never young at all. When she moved to England at the age of nineteen, she found people the same age to be very childish. She herself had been through so much already. The youngsters there had no concept of any of it.

"I don't know if I became an adult immediately after the war," Albert adds, "but I do know I skipped part of my puberty. Normally, you try to liberate yourself from your parents; you start to move away from them when you're about fourteen. But I was in hiding with my parents and my sister at that age, and in that situation, it didn't even occur to me to put distance between them and myself—to discover who I really was. It's what you ought to be doing at that age, but I just wasn't. Not after the war either."

"The fact that you didn't may also have something to do with your personality," Jacqueline notes. "According to her diary, Anne really clashed with her parents. Even without a war, you might not have been so difficult."

"That's quite possible, but looking back, I often thought how I really missed going through that phase."

"You had to be careful not to create any more problems than there already were," Nanette says. "Had there been no war, my adolescence would have proceeded in a very different fashion, I think. But I agree with you, Jacqueline, that Anne fought her parents—especially her mother. And that bothered Otto Frank a lot, don't you think?"

"Absolutely," says Jacqueline. "She really experienced her adolescence fully—no doubt about it. I myself wasn't all that rebellious—rather docile, actually. I didn't offer any opposition, but what I did do was withdraw from my life at home. What I remember very well is that I visited Nanette and Hannah after the war and that I had the unmistakable feeling that the connection between us was gone because they'd had experiences I had not. It gave me a sense of having skipped something. And although our friendship grew again later on, at the time that feeling was very intense."

I fear that the same is true of me. I'd always been extremely conscious of having to be a good little boy at the Van Beeks', which is why I'd never felt the urge to free myself from my parents—there simply was no place for it. In that sense I, too, had skipped my adolescence.

Nanette picks up on my story. "Just like me when I was living with my aunts. I went to London after the war and lived with them for a short while. They were fantastic to me, but I could never really stand up for myself and always had to behave. I had to adapt to them."

THE SUN IS SHINING when the four of us (Lenie has temporarily gone elsewhere) slowly walk over to Anne Frank's former house. The second-floor apartment is now managed by a foundation that offers the space annually to a writer who's being persecuted in his or her own country. Jacqueline happens to know that Anne's former room has been fully restored in the old style and is sorry that we won't be able to see it anymore.

When the group has dispersed, Nanette describes to me how, at some point in 1942, a classmate of hers told her a story. "In Poland, they supposedly had trucks in which they killed people with gas. Such a weird story that I couldn't even believe it."

Putting people to death with gas—a "weird story," indeed, but true nonetheless.

The German Invasion

The beginning of World War II in the Netherlands is well established: a German bombing raid that completely leveled central Rotterdam. The Dutch government was as shocked as the population and, fearing the next attack, surrendered immediately.

Now that we each have the afternoon to ourselves, I take the opportunity to talk at greater length with Albert. I'm curious to hear what he remembers of the day Germany invaded the Netherlands.

"I was sick in bed," Albert says with a smile. "In my parents' big bed, listening to the radio. I remember a report about some German parachutists who'd landed in Rotterdam. I also remember a speech by Queen Wilhelmina condemning the German attack. No one had expected it. In all honesty, I really have no opinion about the queen having left the Netherlands. I suspect she did good work from England; she probably couldn't have done very much had she stayed here. Of course, there are examples of European monarchs who stayed put . . . King Leopold of Belgium. King Christian X of Denmark was very impressive in opposing the Germans: subtle enough so he could stay on as king but clearly on the side of his people, and that was very much appreciated. I never heard anything positive that King Leopold ever did."

When I question Albert about his own reaction to the invasion, he admits that he just couldn't remember. "There wasn't anything anyone could do. After all, the Netherlands could hardly have been expected to fight the Germans, whose army was so much stronger. We surrendered when the heart of Rotterdam had been flattened by the bombs. There were an awful lot of people who tried to escape to England by boat during those last few days, but very few succeeded. I even heard of some people who committed suicide."

Actually, during the first six months of the German occupation, not much changed: it was pretty much business as usual. Sure, your windows had to be blacked out so that pilots couldn't use the light coming from them to navigate—after all, there was no such thing as night vision yet—but other than that, not much was different, Albert says. "Toward the end of that first year, Jewish civil servants were being laid off. Jewish businesses were dispossessed and members of the Dutch Nazi Party were installed as administrators. My father worked for a Jewish company, so the management was dismissed and a group of party members took over. Soon my father was fired as well."

I ask Albert if they ever hid with people who charged them money.

"No, we never paid for being hidden. We were offered hiding places in exchange for a great deal of money. My parents refused those offers, not just because we didn't have that much money but also because we continued to be optimistic. We thought that the war might be over in a few months. We really had no clue that it would last five years. Those people who were offering a hiding place for thousands of guilders a month—truly an awful lot of money then—were obviously only interested in making a profit. We figured they'd inform on us the minute the money was gone. My father was a traveling salesman with many clients, and many good ones among them. He knew whom he could and couldn't trust. At one point, when the money ran out after we'd gone into hiding, we already had made contact with members of the Resistance. My father told me, 'You need to go see so-and-so and ask if they can find any of my former clients who might be willing to help us.' And it worked: every month, some of my father's former clients sent money for us through the Resistance. And they refused to be reimbursed after the war."

I ask if he remembers any of his schoolmates, and who his best friend was.

"That was Leo Slager. He didn't live very far from here; when I rode my bike to the lyceum, I'd pass his house and we'd ride on together from there. I remember one day when we were biking home from school after a German class, I spoke a few German words to him. That infuriated him so much that he made a U-turn and went home by a different route."

Leo Slager didn't survive the war; he was killed in the concentration camp Sobibor.

"My sister lives in America," Albert continues. "A few years ago, some sixty years after the war, she came to the Netherlands. She told me she needed something from the pharmacy—something she couldn't get in America. I took her to the Etos drugstore where she picked up the bottle, looked at the label, read 'Made in Germany,' and immediately put it back again." He looks at me in amazement. "Sixty years after the war."

"You don't have any problems with the Germans anymore?" I ask. "Don't you feel something when you hear German?"

"No, hearing German is no problem for me. Though, I've never visited Germany. Before, when the family and I used to vacation in Switzerland, we'd drive through France—never through Germany."

Escape

The deportations of Jews to Westerbork began two years after the German occupation. At first, notices to go work in the labor camps arrived by ordinary mail. That is what happened to Anne's sister, Margot. She received a summons, and that's when the family decided to go into hiding. It was July of 1942.

"We got the summons on August 1, 1942," Albert says. "For the whole family—my father and mother, my sister, and me. My father wasn't as strong as my mother; he thought he could get out of it by pretending to be ill, but my mother wanted to go underground. It turned into an argument.

"One of my parents' friends had set up a hiding place for himself and his family, just like the Franks. It wasn't far from the Secret Annex. We were able to move in with them. On August 1st, we were notified that we were to appear at Central Station on the fifth, and I believe we went into hiding on the third of August 1942."

When I ask him about his experiences in hiding, he thinks it over for a while. I try to help with questions about food, games, and sports.

"Sports?" He laughs. "That's a good one. My experiences in hiding . . . Our first hiding place was safe for only four months. And we hadn't counted on that. It worked more or less the same way as with Anne Frank: you had people who'd become involved beforehand, who belonged to the organization. They provided food, the most important thing of all by far. Of course, there was an emergency supply that consisted mostly of beans. That could last for a while. A couple of times a week, people would come by with vegetables, fruit, bread, potatoes, and cheese—whatever they could get ahold of. But for that they needed your ration cards, so you also had to have someone get you a ration card at a distribution center. But then those cards were cut off, because the Germans circulated names of individuals who were no longer supposed to be around. Then it was up to you to figure out how to obtain ration cards through the Resistance.

"After that we no longer had a hiding place of our own, but we'd stay with families who did all the shopping for us. We still had to get ration cards, of course, but special shoppers were no longer necessary."

"What did you do most of the time?" I asked.

"We stayed with a friend of my parents at first who was extremely disciplined, so we'd get up early in the morning, seven thirty or eight, and always began the day with calisthenics. I wasn't very good at it, but I dutifully joined in. We always ate three times a day, and on time, too. On the Sabbath—Friday evening and Saturday—Kiddush was made, and after dinner the *bensch*—blessing—would be recited.

"We played Monopoly to entertain ourselves, and the friend also taught me to play chess. My parents played cards endlessly—so much that I learned to play bridge just by watching them. After the war, when I joined a bridge club at school, they let me play competitively right away, although I'd never actually played myself.

"In mid-1943, I ended up in the Gooi region, where it was safe enough for me to go outside. There I could help with the vegetable garden, do the weeding, and occasionally go shopping. Or take walks on the heath with my sister. We had blond hair and fairly light eyes, so we weren't very conspicuous. People may not have even thought I was Jewish. Frankly, I believe that identity is what's inside us."

"Did you ever come close to being caught by the Germans?"

"Yes—four months after we went into that first hiding place, things almost went wrong. It was an old house along the canal with just one front door and a staircase inside that led to several floors. We were downstairs, and above us was a group of artists. They were part of the plot as well, so to speak. They would help us with the shopping and got us ration cards.

"One night, one of the painters was arrested by the Germans and put in jail—not because of us but because he was a Communist. Germany was at war with Russia, and so every Communist was suspect. Apparently, he talked with another prisoner—not with the guards, not with the Germans, but with a fellow prisoner. The artist must have thought he was trustworthy. At some point, the prisoner was set free, and he knew from the painter that we had a stash of food in the house, in case of an emergency.

"One day, he broke in through a secret entrance. The moment that door opened, we thought we were being arrested. That's not what happened, but you can imagine how terrified we were. People who weren't supposed to know we were there evidently did. So it was the ex-prisoner who actually chased us away. I never found out what happened to him afterward.

"Later, in the middle of 1944, we once again barely escaped arrest. We'd just come to the end of our first year in Gooi, in the village of Laren. We knew that most of the police officers there could be trusted, but the mayor was a member of the NSB. We knew that he would go out at night sometimes, hunting for people in hiding.

"One afternoon in June, my parents let my sister and I do the shopping. When we returned, the house was empty. It wasn't only our family that lived there but my uncle's family as well. And normally, the host family was there, too, with their two children. So there were a total of eleven people in that house, but when we came home, there wasn't a soul around.

"It turned out later that the police had come by and found a spinning wheel—the kind used to spin wool. But you weren't allowed to have any wool because all wool was set aside for the German army. If you did have wool, it had to be for the black market and was completely illegal. The police officers had gone over to the spinning wheel and chose to ignore the possibility of anyone hiding in the house. Apparently, they said, 'Next week that spinning wheel has to be gone. We'll be back to check on it.' Those who were there at the time immediately fled, because they understood perfectly well what the officers meant: 'Guys, we're pretending not to see that anyone is in hiding here, but you aren't safe any longer. Because of the mayor, we can't guarantee that everything will work out, so make sure you're gone by next week.' And we managed it, too.

"Then we spent another six months nearby in the village of Eemnes. We lived in a small house whose front door had frosted glass. One day, someone rang the doorbell and through the glass we saw the shape of a man in a black uniform. In those days, anyone in uniform was German and, thus, not to be trusted.

"Because it was the middle of the day, we weren't in our hiding place. We looked at each other and said, 'Trouble.' The seven of us had to get back to our hide-out before one of our hosts could open the door.

"And indeed, it was a man in a Nazi uniform. He said, 'It certainly took a very long time before anyone opened the door, and in the meantime, I heard a lot of thumping around—something's not right here. But I'm not going to risk coming in alone. I'm going to get some backup; then I'll be back.'

"Those really were times when we very narrowly escaped being discovered."

The First Electric Potter in the Netherlands

I tell Albert about my first time building a model airplane. We're slowly wandering around Merwedeplein. I'm curious what he remembers about what children used to do in those strange times.

"As I said, in Laren we also had an uncle, aunt, and cousin of mine move in. So there were seven of us hiding out in a tiny house with only three rooms. Our hosts had two small children themselves and said, 'You can take the largest room, and we'll make do with the other two.'

"We were able to go outside and play in the yard a little. An elderly couple, in their sixties, I guess, lived next to us. They were both artists—potters. Laren was very much an artists' village, where many painters lived, but these two were potters. Every afternoon at five, the man—Mr. Hobbel was his name—would come to the hedge between the two houses. My uncle would be on the other side of the hedge at the same time. Mr. Hobbel secretly listened to English radio broadcasts, which was obviously not allowed since it was enemy radio. All you were allowed to hear was German propaganda. But the English radio brought us news from the other side, and that really gave us hope. Hearing news like that was very encouraging. And every single day, Mr. Hobbel came to the hedge to tell my uncle what he'd heard.

"After the spinning wheel incident, we had to leave. Fortunately, we were able to move in with the sons of the Hobbels. They had a small factory in Eemnes with an electric kiln. That was extremely new then: potters used to stoke their ovens with charcoal, wood, or peat. I was the first one to tend the kiln. They had very precise instructions on how to slowly heat the clay. If you did it too quickly, the pot would crack. The trick was to extract the water from the clay very gradually. So, in 1944, I was the first electric potter in the Netherlands.

"After the war, Mrs. Hobbel gave us a small pot." Albert takes a little square cardboard box from his coat. "I wrapped it very carefully just to be safe," he says, taking the small pot from its thin paper. "I cherish what's still left of it. The lid broke—can't be repaired—and the pot itself has quite a crack as well."

We stare at the little pot, which doesn't look particularly special.

"They can throw it in the garbage when I'm gone." He laughs and carefully wraps it up again.

"Haven't you ever wanted to move to Israel?" I ask.

Albert looks dubious. "Well, I did consider it. But first of all, I don't think I'm tough enough for that difficult country, and secondly, I worried about my parents. My sister had already gone to America, and with the exception of one family member, my parents had lost all their relatives. My father came from a family of ten children. Two brothers survived. Before the war, I had fifteen uncles and aunts; after the war, there were three."

"For some, that's the very reason to leave the Netherlands."

"Yes, I know. I did visit Israel once—a town where other Dutch people lived, but it was a bit stifling. A kind of 'Little Holland.' No, not my thing at all. It was a hard decision, certainly, and there've been times when I regretted not having taken that step. My oldest son lives in Jerusalem now, and that makes me very happy."

"Maybe sometime in the future?"

Albert looks at me as if I'm dim-witted

"THE NUMBER OF PLACES I hid is rather large."

He stares ahead and holds up a hand to start counting. "It started with the house on the canal in Amsterdam. When that went wrong during the Christmas holiday of 1942, we spent some time with my grandmother because the Germans were taking a Christmas break from their persecutions. I was still with her when they started up again, but at night, we'd sleep on the floor of a vegetable store. From there, we moved in with an uncle—he made raincoats, which was useful for the Germans. So he thought he'd be able to hang on for a while. But that fell apart, too, and so we briefly went back to my grandmother's. Then we went to the house of my teacher, from the elementary school now known as the Anne Frank

School. We lived there for four months, or maybe just three. We returned to my uncle's for a very short while and then to Laren where we spent a year. When that didn't work out, we moved to Eemnes for six months to live with the potters' sons. When we had to leave there, we spent a little time with the potters themselves and then returned to Eemnes again. Are we up to eleven different addresses now?" Albert looks at his raised fingers, which he doesn't quite seem to trust. "Oh yeah—somewhere in between I spent one night in Blaricum."

We fall silent for a moment until he suddenly says with a laugh, "I didn't realize what it meant to go into hiding until thirty years after the war. It was because of an older Jewish man who was around eighty and had moved to Eindhoven. I went to pay him a visit on behalf of the Jewish community. After the war, he'd been living in Amsterdam, but he was left alone after his wife died. So he went back to the family that had hidden him during the war and moved in with them.

"What was so terrible about it was that he'd adopted the behavior of someone in hiding again. I had never truly realized what it was actually like, but at that moment, it came as a sudden revelation. When I entered, the man put his fingers to his lips and whispered, 'Shh . . . speak softly and be polite. Everything these people do is right. Don't criticize them, and don't ask for anything.'

"I became terribly anxious and recognized it all: *that* was the feeling of being in hiding. Staying quiet and above all, not wanting anything. Just accepting everything that goes on."

THE FRANK FAMILY HAD HIDDEN in the Secret Annex, a space behind a bookcase that originally was part of the offices of Opekta, Anne's father's company. Thanks to some of Otto Frank's colleagues, the Frank family—together with the Van Pels family and Fritz Pfeffer—was able to remain hidden from the Germans for a few years. I ask Albert whether his father's colleagues were able to do anything for them when they were in hiding.

"Not that I know of," Albert responds after thinking it over for a long time. "Some of his clients, yes. As I told you before, a number of them provided us with money for half of the war. Every single month. There was another client, a very Christian man, whom we'd asked for a place to hide, but he was either unable or unwilling to help. But, needless to say, it's very hard to judge what a person can or cannot do. When my father had just been laid off, there were some clients who gave him a gigantic package with all sorts of household linens: towels, dishcloths, washcloths, and so on. 'That should last you for the rest of the war,' they said, but it was right before we went underground, and we couldn't take all of it with us."

In spite of the restrictions I encountered in hiding, I never really felt I was locked up. Of course, I wasn't locked up at all: I went to school and was free to ride around the neighborhood on my bike. I ask Albert how that was for him; he must have missed those kinds of things terribly.

"Well . . . I think when you're caught up in such a situation, your only concern is to survive. And as long as that works, you're fine." Albert thinks for a moment and then says that he actually never felt all that confined. "The relief of staying out of German hands was enough. Of course, once we were in the Gooi, it was great to be able to go outside again from time to time. I remember that my sister and I were taken to Laren first, before there was any room for my parents. When we arrived, it had been about nine months—from August 1942 until May 1943—that we hadn't been out at all. We looked absolutely awful. Worse, in fact: we looked so ghastly that the people there immediately felt sorry for us and told each other, 'The parents should come, too, because it can't go on this way.' But I never had this oppressive sense of being locked up—not at all."

"Were you able to fall asleep easily while in hiding?"

"Oh, yes. I never had any trouble falling asleep. Our only problem was fleas."

"Or the sound of trains at night?"

"Ah, yes. I almost forgot that location: I was also hiding out in a house in Hilversum right next to the railroad tracks. The first few nights I lay there listening to the sound of passing trains, but then I got used to it and didn't notice it anymore."

"Did you ever get hot food while in hiding?"

"Oh, sure. Usually we had a regular hot meal at night. Except for the last winter of the war, the infamous Hunger Winter; that was a very rough time. In Amsterdam, many people died of starvation that winter. But that had absolutely nothing to do with being underground. In the Gooi region, there was nothing to be had either. For a while, my sister and I would go from door to door to beg. And all we could get was white cabbage so that for six weeks, we ate nothing but cabbage with water.

When my mother wanted to go to sleep at night, she'd complain she was in terrible pain. Her ribs were almost piercing her skin—that's how skeletal she was. Fortunately, however, none of us ever fell seriously ill."

As a young Jewish boy, Albert, too, must have been looking forward to his bar mitzvah. When I ask him about it, his face clouds over.

"Painful topic," he says. "I was in hiding at the time. The last time I cried during the war was on the day that I should have been bar mitzvahed. Thereafter, I didn't cry for decades. Strange phrase, really, going 'underground,' because I was in the attic of a house. Anyway, my grandfather who'd always told me that he really wanted to attend my bar mitzvah had already died of natural causes.

"The day of my bar mitzvah, on a large sheet of paper, I drew all the gifts that I would have wanted to receive had we celebrated the event. At the top was a big bicycle because I'd been forced to turn mine in to the Germans."

"And what did you actually receive in the end?"

"Nothing."

"Nothing?"

"Absolutely nothing."

Hiding in the Forest

What particularly strikes me at this point, even more than I had expected, is how differently each of us has experienced the war. Individual experiences of historical events can vary incredibly widely. The one person with whom I haven't spoken extensively yet is Lenie Duyzend. My conversations with Nanette have led me to believe that Lenie had been in hiding in a forest during the war.

The next day, I get together with her along the Amstel River on the Amsteldijk. Her dark hair is carefully coiffed, the wind barely able to ruffle it. We have a view of the Utrechtse Bridge. From time to time, a small boat passes by, low on the water. These days, loudspeakers are everywhere: the electronic bass booms well beyond the riverbanks, above the roar of the outboard motors.

Lenie describes how she used to ride her bike here as a child.

"In the winter, we sometimes went skating with Anne Frank and a few classmates near where she lived," she says. "Not here on the Amstel but in the section of town they now call the River District. I'm sure that Jacqueline, Hannah, and Nanette must have been there as well."

"What do you remember about that period with Anne?" I ask.

"Well, we laughed a lot. She sat in the front of the class, on the left, by the window—at least, that's what I recall. The teachers laughed a lot with her, too. At first, I thought she was just another nice girl, but later, I began to think she was pretty special.

She began to attract more attention, while at first she was one of many. You and Albert impressed me also. All in all, it was an enjoyable class. And as Jacqueline said before, the poetry album proves that we really didn't have a clue about what awaited us, what plans were in motion. I thought we'd just been assigned to that school for the duration of the war, that it was all just temporary. That everything would then go back to normal."

"Can you remember the first restriction that you faced?"

Lenie doesn't need much time to think. "The first thing was being forced to wear the star. That was followed by Jews no longer being allowed to enter certain places and having to shop in specific stores—at specific hours, in fact. Before we had to wear the star, that was not the case.

"Maybe our radios had to be handed in, but I'm not sure about that. Then we were given the ID card; I think that must have been 1941.

"I suppose we couldn't ride our bikes any longer, because I remember always walking to school with a girlfriend. And I wasn't allowed to use the tram anymore. But the far-reaching restrictions didn't begin until I went into hiding. Because I looked Jewish, I truly had to stay locked up. It was an enormous constraint. The day I went into hiding was a weekday, sometime at the end of May. My parents and I—the three of us. Together, we went to an address on the Beethovenstraat where they stayed, while I was taken around the corner to the Stadionkade where I spent one night. But I was extremely worried, and I had a terrible bellyache. I guess it must have been nerves.

"The following day, someone came to pick me up and took me to the Veluwe region by train, without my star, obviously. I was able to move in with some very nice people and stayed there for a long time. But then there was a raid. Someone had informed on us and said there were Jews hiding there and at other addresses as well.

"In that house, I slept in a kind of closet under the floor. What I mean is, there was a closet in one of the rooms—an ordinary closet with a trapdoor in the bottom. I would go through that and sleep under the floor. They'd close the trapdoor and put pots on top of it, so that way no one could tell there was a person sleeping underneath.

"The raid was truly terrifying; the Krauts came in and demanded the closet be opened. They were barking, 'What else is in there?' Of course, I kept quiet, didn't open my mouth. They didn't know I was there because you couldn't tell from the closet, so they had no idea there was a trapdoor with a bed beneath it.

"As soon as they were gone, I had to rush out—one, two, three—into the rye fields because the wheat was high. I spent several days in one of those fields. Someone brought me food and a blanket. Fortunately, it was July and the weather was good.

"A few days later, they took me in a laundry van somewhere in the Veluwe, in the middle of a dense forest, not far from the towns of Vierhouten and Nunspeet. To my amazement, there were some huts in those thick woods. One small hut was at least three quarters of the way under the ground and very well camouflaged. From a distance, it was absolutely invisible to the untrained eye. I spent a couple of months there; all of Nunspeet helped out. People came by to bring us food: vegetables, bread, potatoes—you name it. Clothing, too. They took really good care of us in that camp. 'The Hidden Village' is what they called it later. At the time, we ourselves called it the 'Be-Careful Camp,' not just because it was appropriate for the situation but because it was located close to the 'Pas-op-weg'—the 'Be-Careful Road.' They said the road took its name from the highwaymen of old who used to terrorize those woods.

"It was an open secret in the village of Vierhouten that people were hiding deep in the forest. Not only Jews, but English and American pilots as well. There was also a Russian and an Italian. And later on, there was a German deserter, too. I remember his arrival. I'd already been there for several weeks or maybe months. Initially, the Jews weren't exactly thrilled with his presence, but in the end, he slept in the same space as I did, together with another family. We had six beds—three bunk beds. Besides, the weather was so nice that we spent the better part of the time in the open air.

"After a while, it became clear that the camp wasn't safe any longer: someone had talked. A few days before, someone from the Resistance had already taken me away on the back of a bicycle, together with a little boy about ten years younger than me. That's how we ended up in Elburg, where we stayed until the end of the war."

So Nanette hadn't been wrong about Lenie hiding in the forest, although I'd been under the impression that she was living in a normal house in the woods. I was reminded of the well-known Polish partisans who used to hide in self-constructed huts in the forest during the war.

I'd fully expected to hear new stories once I got to speak with everyone after all this time, but this was more than I'd anticipated.

A Copied Letter

"Was Anne pretty?" I ask Jacqueline. Because she has devoted years to writing about Anne, she can undoubtedly tell me a lot about the character of our classmate, but first I take the liberty of posing a superficial question.

"I don't think she was pretty or beautiful, but she did have an interesting face." Jacqueline gazes at Merwedeplein where we agreed to meet again today. "She had lovely, very expressive eyes. I don't think I'd call her downright beautiful. The last portrait of her, that school picture where she has her arms crossed, is rather ugly I think, but that's because she's wearing braces, which broaden her face. So I don't really like that picture, although it's appeared all over the world. I doubt she herself would have liked it. There are much nicer pictures of her."

"And what about her personality? Were you alike?" I ask.

"Quite the opposite: we were very different. She was an extrovert, and I was an introvert. This used to cause problems at times. Anne expected me to tell her everything, but I didn't want to, and she chattered all day long and told me almost everything. She decided we were best friends and so we had to tell each other everything. But I didn't consider myself interesting enough to say much."

"Were you as crazy about movie stars as she was?"

"Anne was the collector, and I was the one who helped her clip and glue them. I did like doing that. What I found odd is that she was wild about the stars of the German UFA film studios, with their long blond hair. I simply couldn't understand that at all. Those were the actresses that played in Nazi movies at the time, and so we got to see them in various little newspapers. Marika Rökk and women of her ilk. And Zarah Leander, although she wasn't blond."

From her diary, I envision Anne as a fierce, lively child who often analyzed herself more than people her age usually do. She created reports about her days in the Secret Annex in letters to an imaginary friend named Kitty. Real letters from Anne to real people are rare—not surprisingly, for she couldn't send any from her hiding place. One letter to Jacqueline has survived. It is a farewell letter that Anne wrote her just before she surreptitiously left with her family for the Secret Annex.

Jacqueline puts on her reading glasses and reads me the good-bye letter. The letter has been included in its entirety in Jacqueline's books *My Name Is Anne, She Said, Anne Frank* and *Anne and Jopie.* Anne signed the letter "your 'best' friend, Anne." The hopeful postscript states, "I trust we'll be 'best' friends until we see each other again."

"She wrote me this letter just before she went into hiding," Jacqueline says. "We had agreed that if one of us had to go, we would write each other—except that she wasn't allowed to send it or have it delivered by hand. I didn't get the letter until her father gave it to me after the war. Once it was known that his two daughters wouldn't be coming back, Miep Gies returned the diary and all of Anne's papers to Otto Frank. That's when he found the letters, because Anne had copied them in her diary. There's another letter to me in her diary.

"'Thanks for your letter,' she writes. It's written as a response to a letter of mine, but I never wrote the one she refers to because I had no idea where she was at that moment. Those who knew her thought she was in Switzerland because Otto Frank had left a note behind with a Swiss address—on purpose, so people wouldn't think the family had gone underground. Throughout the whole war, I had no idea where she was, so I never wrote back to her. But when she'd copied that letter, she apparently imagined I'd answered her."

"When was the last time you spoke with Anne?" I ask.

"It was the Sunday evening before they went into hiding on Monday. We phoned each other. It was a perfectly ordinary conversation. I never had the feeling it would be the last time. I guess we talked about everyday things—I don't really remember: homework, school."

Because of what Jacqueline told me the day before, I already know she escaped persecution in a very special way. It's actually a story of boundless maternal love, combined with an unimaginable amount of courage, and I tell her that I'd really like to hear it again.

Jacqueline smiles and starts with the meeting of her parents, when everything began.

"My father was a Jew from Amsterdam and my mother a Catholic from Paris who'd come to Amsterdam to work," she says. "My mother fell instantly in love with my father. At first, she didn't want to stay in the Netherlands, so when my father—who was just as smitten with her—proposed to her, she basically fled back to France. My father followed his heart and moved his business to Paris. That's where they were married and, at my father's request, my mother converted to Judaism, and that's where my sister was born as well. Later, my father really wanted to return to the Netherlands, and so they came back. I was born here, in 1929."

"Was your father's Jewish heritage ever a problem before the war broke out?"

"My mother was concerned about her parents' reaction, for she knew that her father—like most

French people at the time—wasn't wild about Jews. But my father adjusted easily to his parents-in-law, who liked him right away. He spoke French perfectly, had lived in Paris for a few years, so it all went very smoothly, although his being Jewish sometimes did become a topic of conversation.

"It may surprise you, but my father's family's attitude toward my mother was a far greater problem. My father's side was heavily Orthodox, and they found that Catholic woman rather strange: she didn't speak Dutch well, and although my mother really did her utmost to obey Jewish customs—a tablecloth and candle on the table on Friday evening—she wasn't fully accepted. I could see that already when I was small. My father's brothers had two daughters, and those girls were more readily accepted than my sister and me. It was very obvious. Strange perhaps, but there were more problems in the other direction."

"How did you think of yourself—Catholic or Jewish?"

"I didn't feel Catholic, for that wasn't part of my life at home at all. I felt somewhat Jewish—half Jewish. Occasionally, I'd go to the synagogue with my father. I should add that when my father married my mother, he wasn't terribly religious anymore and didn't observe Jewish customs that much. That changed later on. During the war, he became extremely devout, which caused my parents to grow apart."

"Were you closer to your father or your mother?"

"My mother was a very domineering person, so I tended to do what she wanted, but that's not the same as being close to someone, I suppose. I later resisted Mother's coercion. My father died in 1952, and in the postwar years, my parents had many marital problems. Around that time, I withdrew from both of them—from my father, too. A complicated tale, as you see."

"Why did they actually send you to the lyceum? You weren't really Jewish, after all."

"Aha," Jacqueline answers. "That's true, but as I mentioned yesterday, it's how we were thought of by the Germans—another complicated story. My mother had converted to Judaism in Paris. In 1928, my parents returned to the Netherlands. The Orthodox Jewish community wouldn't acknowledge my mother because they thought the Parisian rabbi was far too liberal. My father, who really wanted my sister and me to be Jewish, had to ensure that my mother would be acknowledged as a Jew by the Jewish community, but it took them many years to agree to that. I don't know how he managed in the end, but in 1938, he did succeed. My mother was recognized, and so my sister and I became Jewish. My father was very happy because he didn't want it just for himself alone but also for his family in France.

"It really wasn't very good timing. The Germans arrived in 1940. You had to declare the origins of your grandparents, but the anti-Jewish laws didn't apply—not yet anyway—if there were only one or two Jewish grandparents. But they did apply if you were registered with the Jewish community. So the Nazis considered my sister and me to be Jews, which is why I had to attend the lyceum despite the fact that I had only two Jewish grandparents. That created quite a few complications.

"At some point, my mother realized the nature of the threat. And she *did* believe the rumors that were going around. That's when she swung into action. She told one highly placed intelligence officer, 'My husband registered me with the Jewish community without my knowledge.' It wasn't true, of course, but that's what she said to the man. 'So now my children are Jewish, too, and I want you to undo that.' She told him this in French because she had made sure she'd see someone who spoke French. She used all her charm: she had dressed up, worn a hat, and made a real impression on him.

"'If you can provide us with the birth and baptismal certificates of both your grandparents, we'll believe you and we'll make sure your children's names will be deleted from the deportation list,' the officer told her.

"In the end, that became an incredibly drawn-out affair because the papers had to come from the south of France, which at the time wasn't occupied by the Germans. But it worked, and by the end of 1942, we were able to take the yellow star off our clothes and have our names disassociated from the Jewish community, which is how we were removed from the deportation list."

"Did your father go along with all of this as well?"

"When my mother told us of her plan, we had to promise her not to tell my father. That upset me a lot because I really didn't like doing that. But I had to. My father knew nothing about it until almost the last moment when my mother finally told him. They had a big fight. It so happened that my father was very optimistic and thought the war would soon be over. He didn't believe what he heard would happen to the Jews, and it *was* really incredible, of course. My mother had already mentioned gassing, and I clearly remember her warning my father's family when they stopped by one day: 'You should go underground, or they will gas you,' she cried out. I didn't grasp what she was talking about, but I was only eleven.

"My uncle, the husband of my father's sister, never cared much for my mother and gave her a piece of his mind: 'How did you come up with that! That's just hogwash; of course we're going.' They'd already been summoned. 'We'll have to work hard, but if we go into hiding and are discovered, then we'll be in real trouble. They'll punish us, and everyone knows that means certain death.'

"So they didn't go underground, and they never came back from the camps. My father had two sisters and three brothers, and all of them and their children died in the camps."

We're quiet for a moment. I conclude that Jacqueline's life was in fact saved by her mother's bold action.

"Not only my life and that of my sister, but my father's as well, for after 1943 he, too, was able to take off the yellow star. There were hardly any Jews in Amsterdam anymore. The remaining Jewish wives were forced to be sterilized so the Germans could ensure no other Jewish children would be born. Fortunately, Amsterdam had doctors who were willing to issue a false declaration, and my father obtained one of these as well."

"Were you ever angry that your mother so forcibly denied she was Jewish?" I ask. It must be quite something to refute one's faith.

The Montessori School in Amsterdam, known today as the Anne Frank School. (Photograph courtesy of Sidney Brandeis)

The Jewish Lyceum in Amsterdam, present day. The building is currently used as a beauty and hairdressing school, but the exterior has remained largely the same since before World War II. (Photograph courtesy of Sidney Brandeis)

Theo Coster as a young boy in the Montessori school. (Photograph courtesy of the author)

Theo Coster (standing to the right) inside of Hadera Papermills in Israel, where he worked during the 1960s. (Photograph courtesy of the author)

The former site of the Westerbork concentration camp, where Hannah Goslar briefly reunited with Anne. (Photograph courtesy of the author)

Today Westerbork contains a Holocaust memorial composed of 102,000 tiny pillars—one for each person who died at the camp. (Photograph courtesy of the author)

"No, not in the least, for I knew she was saving my life by doing that. It was such a frightening time that I was incredibly happy when I could remove the star. I stayed at the lyceum until December 1942. Things had only just begun then. It was only kids sixteen or seventeen years old that they picked up, allegedly to be sent to work. That was followed by the raids, which were extremely upsetting, and I was scared it would happen to us as well. So I thought my mother had been very clever to get us deleted from the Jewish register. At first, my father was quite angry, but he later realized that it had saved his life, too."

Visiting the Anne Frank House

At seven in the morning the next day, Lenie, Nanette, and I pay a visit to the Anne Frank House. We have been given permission to arrive before regular opening hours, before the tourists who line up daily. The museum has more than a million visitors a year and sometimes as many as three hundred in a single hour. As we enter, I realize it's my first time here; a visit is certainly overdue.

We look at the scale models of the different floors of the premises that included the Secret Annex as well. Lenie resolves to read the book again. "I came here in 1945 or 1946 with Miep [Gies] to visit

Otto Frank, when it wasn't a museum yet. Later on, I figured there was no need to see it as a museum; I'd been here when it was just the Annex, after all."

She thinks back to the time she spent in the woods and, glancing at the model of the famous hiding place, she mumbles, "Being locked up in a city is much worse. The occupants of the Secret Annex were really one on top of the other."

Hand in hand, we slowly go up the stairs. An old Opekta poster hangs on the wall. We reminisce about mothers who made their own jam. I happen to know that pectin is especially important for making strawberry jam, because apples and berries, for instance, already have plenty of pectin naturally. One learns the oddest things in life.

We enter a room that has an excerpt from Anne's diary on the wall. "'July 11 1942 . . . We are very nervous that the neighbors might hear us or see something going on,'" Lenie reads out loud. "So that was four weeks after her birthday," she observes. "As for me, I wasn't allowed to make noise either at my various locations. Not even in that hidden camp in the Veluwe woods. Fire lanes divided the forest into squares so that in case of a fire, not everything would be lost. Obviously, there were rules: we weren't allowed out of the forest, and we weren't allowed to walk in the fire lanes because then we might be seen.

And we weren't allowed to make too much noise in the woods. Remaining quiet was more difficult for the English and American pilots who'd crashed and been welcomed into the camp. However, our situation wasn't anywhere nearly as hard as Anne's."

We go on upstairs, to the Opekta offices of Otto Frank, and then to his room, which is closed to the public because the original furnishings are still there. Everything is in perfect condition and decorated in brown.

"So this is where they listened to the BBC," Nanette says, standing in front of the small square radio. Beside it is a framed print of Frankfurt, the city from which the Frank family originated.

"And where's that famous chestnut tree, then?" Lenie asks, walking straight to the window of the room.

"Didn't it come down?" I ask. The news had spread as far as the living rooms in Israel that the celebrated tree mentioned in Anne's diary had begun to rot on the inside and wouldn't last much longer.

Lenie tells us that it had looked as if the tree would have to be cut down but the idea had been thrown out. And, to be sure, the tree's still there, surrounded by a kind of metal corset. According to Lenie, the current plan is to plant a shoot of the tree in the same spot when the time is right.

"A beautiful idea," Nanette says, "but I won't be around to see it."

The three of us look at the old chestnut tree that, unbeknownst to itself, has become a historic heritage simply because Anne Frank would sometimes look at it.

"When I was in hiding," Lenie says, "I, too, used to love looking out, especially in the spring when nature came to life again."

I would go swimming, I think, but this doesn't seem like the right moment to mention that.

Then we go into the room where the jam was made. We study the old-fashioned food mills; the soap fibers, a "detergent for cleaning wool," I read; the jars with spices; the scales; and the bottles of pectin.

In another room, Lenie recalls a frightening moment.

"I was in Oosterwolde, in the house on the Winterdijk, before my time in the camp in the forest. In Oosterwolde, I was with some very nice people who occasionally allowed me to take a little walk after the sun went down.

"One day, some work had to be done inside the house. The workmen were busy in the hallway, and I had to hide or else they'd see me and it would soon be clear that I was a Jew in hiding. I hid in the corner between the hearth and my bed.

"I sat there for hours, on my knees, out of sight from the workmen. I could barely move and soon started getting cramps.

"At a certain point, I hadn't heard any more thumping for a long time, no more talking, no more breathing—nothing. I assumed the coast was clear, at least momentarily. I cautiously raised myself from my tight little spot, and at that very second, the door opened. I was looking straight into the eyes of a man standing on the threshold looking at me. It scared me to death, but luckily, it all ended well.

"It was the only day that anyone ever worked inside the house. Normally, I could do what I wanted and be in the yard."

"And how did you spend your time?" I ask.

"I studied the usual subjects, such as math and English. German, too. I received letters from my parents who were in hiding in different places. Once I'd read the letter, it was torn up because it did happen that saved letters could betray people. Letters from parents to children would become a death sentence. So saving them was not allowed."

We go up a steep staircase that leads to the Secret Annex. It is an effort for me to push aside the heavy bookcase—something we've been given permission to do—behind which is the entrance to Anne Frank's hiding place. We go into the room that Otto, his wife, and Margot used as a bedroom. Adjoining it is Anne's room, of which I already have an image, based on her diary descriptions.

Pictures of movie stars are glued to the wall, behind protective glass now, among whom I recognize Shirley Temple and Greta Garbo. There are reproductions of Leonardo da Vinci as well.

"Shirley Temple," Lenie says. "I was crazy about her."

"Do you remember the film *One Hundred Men and a Girl?*" I ask. She does.

When Lenie goes over to the height marks on the wall, possibly the most famous lines of this kind in the world, we conclude that Anne wasn't short. "When she was in class with us, she was a lot shorter, I believe," Lenie remarks. The message the lines convey is clear: Anne's life behind the boarded-up windows of the Secret Annex went on as usual.

For the tenants of the Secret Annex, the raid on August 4, 1944, by the SD—the German Secret Service—consisting of three inspectors and senior squad leader Karl Silberbauer, meant the end of their time in hiding. They were given a few minutes to pack some clothes and were then taken by car to the SD headquarters on the Euterpestraat, near the very location where Jacqueline's mother had argued to save her family's life. From there, they were transported to the House of Detention on the Weteringschans. On the morning of August 8, they were put on a train to Westerbork, from where they were to be deported to a concentration camp as "punishment."

The identity of the person who betrayed the Frank family has never come to light. It is suspected that it was one of the warehouse workers, but the individual in question has always denied it.

The museum section upstairs in the Secret Annex contains photographs of Auschwitz. I have to admit I've never looked at these horrific images. Only now does it truly register with me how all-encompassing the whole thing was. They show a film, too, in which Hannah Goslar speaks, and so now, after two weeks, I get another glimpse of her.

From Westerbork, Anne was sent to Auschwitz where, during the selection on the platform, they decided she wouldn't go to the gas chamber. A few months later, when both Anne and Margot were very ill and weak, they were sent on to the dirty, chaotic camp of Bergen-Belsen.

In the video, Hannah describes how she went looking for Anne in the camp. "If she had known that her father was still alive . . ." she says. She supposes that in that case, Anne might have hoped to be reunited with him and maybe would have survived the war.

In Bergen-Belsen, Anne was able to withstand typhoid and unimaginable deprivation for a good four months. She died in March 1945, a few weeks before the Liberation. She was fifteen years old.

NANETTE IS STANDING IN FRONT of the photographs of Auschwitz, saying that, in light of all she knows about it, it's not easy for her to look at them. Her memories of that camp are powerful.

"And the pictures don't reflect everything either," she says, troubled. "The air, the stink, the whole atmosphere. They don't show the fear, the sounds. As I look at these pictures, everything comes back to me. The piles of corpses. My father died there, and my mother and brother left there. I stayed behind, alone.

"Like almost everyone, I was undernourished and emaciated. In the sanatorium, after eating for several weeks, I still weighed almost nothing."

Nanette tells us that in the camp, they had to stand for roll call, sometimes for hours. "There are images you can't possibly imagine if you haven't seen them with your own eyes. When the war was nearing its end—which we began to sense because of the increasing number of allied planes overhead—the guards were growing extremely uneasy. Once, I was standing in line to get water when a guard pulled me out. He wanted to shoot and kill me. I didn't care anymore at all: I was alone, my father had already died, my mother and brother had been taken away. I think I must have stood there looking so befuddled that any excitement about killing me must have left him. To feel some release, he just shot into the air."

Afterward, Nanette admits to me that she still has nightmares. "Anyone who spent any time there was scarred. You can't shut off your brain, and without wanting them, memories re-emerge at the strangest moments. You have to learn to live with it; there's nothing you can do."

We go down to the archives in the cellar. A staff member of the Anne Frank House has something she wants to show me. She takes a small round box from one of the many filing cabinets. Carefully, she puts on white rubber gloves before taking a little notebook from the box. It has a hard cover, and many pages are blank. I watch over her shoulder. Reaching a specific page, she stops flipping through them.

"Aha," I call out. "Freddy Coster." That's my sister. I sit down and read on. "'Dear Edith, little acts of love / tender gentle words / have often to the smallest house / delivered greatest bliss. Your classmate, Freddy Coster.' In a corner of the page, she added, 'I forgot the date, as the mice ate the calendar. Bye now!'"

"And here's the little poem by Margot," the woman says. She continues flipping through.

"Who was Edith actually? A classmate?"

"Yes. Edith Jacobson was a classmate at the Jekerschool. She was originally from Berlin, which is why the earlier poems are in German. Then she came to Amsterdam and her classmates wrote in Dutch, of course."

"Is she still alive?"

"We don't know. I do have another notebook from the Montessori School in which you are mentioned, too."

A few moments later, I'm looking wistfully at the small and beautiful old notebooks. Marvelous clear handwriting, all written with dip pen.

The three of us are given special permission to visit the backyard. The gravel crunches under our feet as we walk to a little pond covered in duckweed. Children's laughter from the endless line at the museum's entrance reaches us as a gentle buzzing. It's another magnificently bright day: the weather is unusual for the Netherlands. The sun gleams on the windows of the surrounding houses, while the mighty chestnut tree towers above it all. If trees could think, it would surely be wondering what all these little old people below are up to.

Westerbork

Nanette, her husband John, and I are visiting the former transit camp Westerbork. Today, it bears the name "Memorial Camp Westerbork." It is from here that more than a hundred thousand Jews and Gypsies were sent on to German concentration camps. Knowing that the Dutch government was responsible for building this camp still leaves a bad taste in my mouth. Before the Second World War broke out, a great many German Jews had already fled to other countries, including the tolerant Netherlands. Because the Netherlands wanted to remain on friendly terms with Germany, it closed its borders on December 15, 1938, and declared that henceforth, all Jewish refugees were illegal aliens. Camp Westerbork was built especially for them, so that a few years later, it was simply taken over by the Nazis.

We walk through a wooded area, following a long footpath. Sumptuous lawns give the place a parklike feeling. Your first impression is not one of the atrocious things that happened here during the war, although in this case, they have left their traces: still visible are the railroad tracks, over which prisoners in cattle cars were transported to Auschwitz.

"I remember these tracks very clearly," Nanette says, "and the mayhem of the people departing on Tuesday mornings because, in my opinion, they were quite conscious of the fact that something was very much amiss. If you ask me, it's these tracks that destroyed the Jewish community, and not its body as much as its soul. Gradually, people were beginning to grasp that what they'd been told was untrue. They weren't being sent to labor camps at all. Besides, children and the elderly aren't needed in any labor camp. So it was no surprise that the people here had a sense of impending doom."

I ask if she still remembers the day she first arrived here.

"I arrived on September 29, 1943. We came on a regularly scheduled train from the Amsterdam station. On February 15, 1944, we were transported to Bergen-Belsen, again on a regular train because we had Palestine certificates. It was their intention to exchange us for prisoners of war," she explains. "I don't really recall how long the trip to Westerbork was. All

I remember is barracks—no trees. It looks like an attractive park now, but it was a grim field then. The barracks, the barbed wire, the train, the anxiety, and the conditions in which we were living—it was all very depressing. Granted, there were a lot of people, but the majority were in absolute despair because they were afraid they'd be deported."

"What was your family's reaction when they heard you'd been summoned?"

"They were extremely worried, but there was nothing left to do. We were told we were going to Bergen-Belsen, a destination we thought better, for it was a *Sternenlager,* a star camp. That's what the Germans called it to keep the Red Cross at bay. People were held there who later might be used for exchange. It was considered to be one of the better camps. And indeed, it wasn't an extermination camp, but the conditions were so terrible that the inmates often died anyway." Nanette is visibly affected by her own words.

"What did they feed you in Westerbork?" I ask.

"I don't really remember what we had to eat. I have an image of myself next to an oven because we had to prepare our own food. I can't recall the menu, but there was a little bread, so we didn't die of starvation. That came later, in Bergen-Belsen."

We pass a field of flowers—lupines. They're almost unseemly in their beauty at this time of year.

Nanette follows my gaze. "In sixty years, they've had time enough to turn it into a lovely park, haven't they? I wouldn't recognize it as Camp Westerbork anymore."

We visit the area where the disciplinary barracks used to be. It's hard to know whether they are the original ones or not. To be honest, it makes little difference to me. The shacks stand behind a double fence of barbed wire. This is where they held Anne Frank because she'd been in hiding and for that reason was assigned to the barracks as punishment.

"She, too, must have been told she was going to be a lot worse off in Auschwitz than people in the standard barracks," Nanette says, "but in the end, it was all the same anyway. What a farce."

I ask whether there was any form of recreation in these barracks.

"Yes, there were a few things. I guess some of that should be inside the museum. There was singing, and the children were kept especially busy. Considering the constantly changing population here, it's astonishing that anything was actually organized at all. If my memory serves me right, we were allowed to receive packages, too.

"Incidentally, my mother caught lice pretty early on. I know she was mortified, but she could do nothing about it, nor could she have prevented it. There was no remedy for lice. Perhaps there were drugs available if you were sick, but I never used any of them—although I almost blacked out once. That must have been the beginning of my malnourishment; I was fourteen, after all—a growing girl.

"As for personal care, I can only remember the so-called latrines where you'd use the bathroom and wash your hands. I imagine the hygiene wasn't exactly of a high caliber, which might explain my mother's lice.

"Because of the lice, they made me burn my clothes, though I'd been allowed to keep them throughout my time at the camp, thanks to the Palestine certificates. I tried to keep myself clean as best I could and pick the lice off my clothing. It's impossible to prevent that kind of pest, of course, and everyone had them."

Somewhere in a field not far from the path stands the remainder of a barracks. The walls are made of cement slabs, and the cracks between them are visible. It's easy to imagine how horribly cold it must have been in the winter. I hardly dare reflect on all the luck I had with my refuge during the war years.

NEAR THE REMNANTS of another barracks, a dozen yards further along, a guide is explaining the conditions in the camp to a group of eleven- or twelve-year-olds and their parents. I find it rather extraordinary that children of this age are interested. When the guide has finished her story, I can't contain myself and ask her permission to pose a question to the group, which she grants.

"I'd like to know why you and your parents, who are also still young and for whom Westerbork is no more than a piece of history either, have come all this way from the center of Amsterdam?"

A boy in a green T-shirt looks up at me and answers with a slight accent: "First of all, we're not from Amsterdam." He turns around and goes back to an untied shoelace. A "secondly" remains suspended in the air.

"We're from Geleen," a small boy adds timidly. With a little urging from one of the adults behind him, he admits that he finds it "interesting" and "useful."

When I explain that Nanette and I were classmates of Anne Frank, everyone, even the boy with the shoelace, turns to us attentively. I clarify that we're as old as Anne would have been: eighty. Nanette tells them that she was imprisoned here before she was deported to Bergen-Belsen. As she describes her meeting with Anne, an adorable little girl with huge sunglasses takes a picture of us.

When one of the children's chaperones remarks how miraculous it is that Nanette survived it all, Nanette smiles in agreement.

"Indeed," she says. "It's one of the reasons I'm here: people may not be able to believe it, but they should know that it really happened. What we had here was a 'killing machine'—not just part of a normal war, but a killing machine. We shouldn't forget this past, and we must remain informed about what's happening today. What went on then should never happen again."

When the conversation comes to an end, we bid the group good-bye. The guide adds one more thing, about the menu in Westerbork—something we've been curious about ourselves—which must have been extremely limited. A lot of beets, probably. Enough, most likely, but still very limited. Very little protein, and certainly no meat.

"May I take a picture with you?" a tall girl in a Smurf-blue T-shirt asks Nanette. Before Nanette can respond, the girl throws her arms around my gray-haired friend and is immortalized by a classmate.

As we walk on, Nanette continues her narrative. She has a lot more to say about the camp, and the site is large enough for all her stories. She tells us they used to sleep in bunk beds, on something that vaguely resembled a thin little mattress. Her duties consisted of guarding the camps and assisting the Germans.

"That's when I became aware that those Germans also had families they needed to take care of, and yet it still didn't stop them from participating in these atrocities."

We pass the remains of a washroom shed. Inside, an enormous stone slab about sixty centimeters (twenty-four inches) thick is suspended at knee height. It contains holes with a radius of thirty centimeters (twelve inches) each.

"So these were the toilets we just mentioned," Nanette says. "Also known as the latrine." With barely concealed revulsion, she walks around the stone contraption.

"It was revolting. Always horribly filthy. Diarrhea . . ."

We quickly move on. She turns around one more time to look at the last barracks.

COUNTLESS BIRDS ARE AROUND US, singing loudly. Children are sitting on the grass on either side of the path, listening to a teacher or a guide.

Nanette wants to see the monument, so that's where we're heading.

"Did you ever run into a familiar face while you were here?" I ask when we reach the artwork that stands where roll call used to take place. "Classmates perhaps?"

We're studying the 102,000 stones that symbolize the number of victims of Westerbork.

"Not classmates, but acquaintances, yes. In the first place, we were mostly concerned with ourselves, of course. How could we manage to survive under these circumstances, in these uncertain times? It's probably hard to imagine what it's like to wait for a summons for deportation every week. To be deported for good."

"Did you have any knowledge of the concentration and extermination camps?"

"No, we children really didn't know anything about that. Whether my parents had their suspicions . . . I truly don't know. Perhaps. Yes, probably, for there was a tendency to resist those departures for Bergen-Belsen. The possibility of registering for the Palestine list originated with my father's bank, the Bank of Amsterdam, which thought it could protect its employees and their families that way. You could only sign up for a short period of time; it consisted of a select group, but if you ask me, I don't think it actually amounted to anything at all."

Expunging Memories

We've reached the Westerbork Museum. On a scale model of the camp, Nanette shows us where her barracks stood, and we see the latrine whose remains we just passed.

"Looking at it now, it couldn't have been that hard to escape," Nanette observes. "But we certainly weren't aware of it at the time."

I note there were barracks for men, for women, for work, for school, and for the sick. "Service places, private buildings," I read aloud in English.

"And that was the orphanage," Nanette points out. "Do you know the story of Truus Wijsmuller-Meijer?" Nanette asks. "She went to the Gestapo to explain the plight of the little children here, who themselves didn't even know who they were, and certainly not where they were. They'd probably come with their parents who'd been picked up by the Germans but had no documents. They called them 'unknown children.' They wore a tag around their neck that said 'UNKNOWN CHILD.'

"Truus went to the Gestapo and said, 'These children are the products of relationships between

German soldiers and Jewish girls. So you can't send them to the death camps because they're part of you.' Whether they believed her or not, the fact is these kids were held back at Westerbork. In the end, they were transported to Bergen-Belsen and then to Theresienstadt. Forty-eight or forty-nine of them survived, thirty of whom were later tracked down."

Before this rescue operation, Truus Wijsmuller-Meijer had already saved thousands of Jewish children; she'd succeeded in getting many young refugees to Great Britain even before the occupation.

"And here is where they held roll call; we had to stand at attention while they counted us. Five in a row. It seemed to go on for an eternity. And all too often, that was the case. You know, I've never really understood why we had to be counted—and so frequently, at that. Most of the time, they had to do a recount as well. It probably had something to do with the trains they had to fill. Inconceivable, isn't it? It really was an operation on an industrial scale.

"In the sanatorium where I spent many years after the war, I ran into a girl who'd been liberated from Auschwitz just when she was in the gas chamber. The Russians got her out. The personnel in charge had already fled or had just been arrested. I also heard a story about a woman from Poland who was taken from the gas chamber because there were more people in there than the Germans considered necessary."

A sign informs us that the conversion of Westerbork into a commemorative museum was carried out under the direction of Ralph Prins, one of the camp's survivors.

I ask Nanette to describe what the average camp inmate looked like.

"Bergen-Belsen or Westerbork?"

"Was there a difference?"

"Bergen-Belsen was divided into separate sections. They were in fact different small camps. I never wore a uniform there. We had to take ice-cold showers, but I was never tattooed, my hair was never shaved, and I always wore my own clothes. Other people had uniforms—striped uniforms. I guess that's why I've hated stripes all my life. Every person was classified separately. Certain prisoners had to work, and the most prestigious job was helping in the kitchen. If you worked there, they wouldn't randomly shoot and kill you."

"What did you look like?"

"By the end of the war, I looked like a skeleton. My hip bones were poking through my skin. They weighed me when I'd already been in the sanatorium for a while, and I was thirty-two kilos, barely seventy pounds. So I must have weighed a lot less before. Like all women who are undernourished, I no longer had my period. A woman menstruates as part of the human reproductive process, but we were in no shape to produce anything whatsoever. If I'm not mistaken, I didn't start to get my period again until I was seventeen, so it took more than a year before everything went back to normal and to gain back the weight at which I would be able to have children. I'm telling you this to give you an idea of the state I was in."

That's when I remember the stories I once read about the liberation of the camps. Prisoners weren't just cadaverous; the lack of food had also shrunk their stomachs. Unbeknownst to themselves or the liberators, food and drink were now life-threatening. There are innumerable cases of liberated prisoners who were provided with meat, bread, and water by the Allied soldiers but who died anyway because their bodies were unable to digest the food. How ghastly that must have been for all concerned.

When I ask what she thought the reason for her own survival was, she shakes her head. "No one can answer that. Why, why not . . . spotted fever could be survived only in theory, but miraculously, I also made it through pleurisy and tuberculosis. I must have enjoyed better-than-average good health in my youth. There were plenty of times that my family didn't expect me to make it."

"Would Anne have survived if she'd been stronger?"

"Impossible to say, of course, but I think not. She looked incredibly frail. Typhoid is such a serious, destructive disease—when you're that weak to begin with, it's impossible to survive. I don't believe her chances of making it through had to do with her willpower; after all, everyone *wants* to survive. That hope is there until the end. And like everyone else she, too, wanted to live."

"Were you able to talk about any of this right after the war?" I ask carefully.

"No," she says decisively. "Perhaps I could have with my family in England, but I think not even with them. They thought it would be better for my recovery—both physically and spiritually—if I left my wartime experiences behind. So as far as that was concerned, I had to cope on my own. There was no facility that could offer psychological support, either; you just had to figure it out for yourself.

"I think this terrible period of uncertainty and fear must affect every person differently. Many probably reached a point where they told themselves, 'Fine, now we want to forget about it, so let's not discuss it anymore.' They imagined they could go on with their life without these memories. It seems easier to expunge them, but I believe the brain doesn't have a delete function—it only has a memory key. You remember things at the strangest moments and without any provocation. That's how deeply it's embedded. I'm sure it's the same for everyone."

In the museum, we're allowed to visit the archives accompanied by one of the staff members. We wander through the rows of shelves that can hold their own with the average university library's language section. Our guide stops at a cabinet and pulls out lists of names from one of the archives. He hands one to Nanette, who, within a few seconds, finds her own name. For tangible proof of that unspeakable time, she is allowed to take a copy home.

part 3

After the War

(Age Seventeen)

Sometime in April, we found out through the radio that the Allies were approaching. Where, how many, when and what was happening, or how soon wasn't very clear yet, but it was a foregone conclusion for everyone that something was afoot. That same month, we suddenly heard a motorcyclist pass by during the daytime. It just had to be a Canadian, for as I recall, the Germans were the only ones using motorized vehicles, especially toward the end of the war. The Allies had control of Dutch airspace and, thus, knew that anything on the roads was likely German, and from their planes, they'd generally aim their machine guns at every car or other motor vehicle.

But the sound of this motorist wasn't accompanied by the firing of a gun or the roar of a plane. No one shot at him—not from the ground or from the air. He was riding on the Zwolseweg, a long road from Zwolle to Apeldoorn lined with small villages.

It was April 17, 1945.

One Canadian on a motorcycle—just one man, in the distance, on a motorcycle.

I didn't see him, since he drove along the main road while I was on a side-street—I just heard him softly, along with the cheering that accompanied the distant drone of the motor. That was the Liberation: the sound of a motorcycle passing in the distance.

The relief that we felt is beyond comparison. It was superb: that never-ending, ceaseless, rotten war had finally come to an end! Marvelous, tremendous, divine. We must have danced with happiness, and if we'd had anything with which to celebrate, we would have held the greatest party of all time—for days or even weeks. But at that time, we didn't have anything.

During the days that followed, the Canadians would sometimes give us white bread—something we hadn't seen for years and certainly not tasted. And they gave us chocolate, too. It was as if the liberators were bringing their own modest banquet with them. But after all those years of misery, each little morsel tasted better than the next and there was nothing modest about it.

In those blissful weeks, I also saw some young women who had been "friendly" with German soldiers and had their heads shaved, right there in the middle of the street. For everyone to see.

RIGHT AFTER THE LIBERATION, our family was assigned a house on the edge of Vaassen. It was a wooden house, occupied by a member of the NSB during the war. My father had joined us again, too, and we lived there as a family for several months. During that period, my father would occasionally go back and forth to check on what was left of Amsterdam and our old apartment. We were dreading it because we knew that after all that time, we'd better not count on anything.

During the Nazi occupation, the moving company Puls had been ordered to clear out all the homes of arrested Jews or those Jews who had escaped. Furniture and other personal possessions were redirected to a new non-Jewish recipient or shipped to Germany. Soon, such clearances became known as "pulsing." Our place was not pulsed because our neighbor Mr. Van Straten had paid our rent throughout the war years.

At first during the war, my father had simply continued to pay the rent, even though none of us were living there, but as time went on, he stopped and no one sent him a bill.

After the Liberation, he still had the house key. He must have been utterly amazed and thrilled when he arrived at our place to find that not only had it survived the war intact, but nobody had even tried to force the lock. And the key still worked. Additionally, not only was all the furniture still there—most of it weighing a ton and indestructible—but all the silverware and dish sets were complete and in place. The photo albums still stood side by side in rows on the bookcase. It was extraordinary: there are countless stories of the plundering of homes abandoned by escaping Jews. Not only did the Germans frequently confiscate Jewish household effects, but neighbors and acquaintances of those in hiding had a habit of appropriating them as well. In an occupied city where an antique clock might mean two days' worth of food, you couldn't expect to leave your belongings behind unattended.

My parents' marriage certificate hadn't been discovered, which would undoubtedly have shown that they'd had a *chuppah,* the traditional Jewish wedding ceremony. A single glance would have proven that I had four Jewish grandparents—not two. Had the Germans discovered that marriage certificate, there's no doubt that I, too, would have had the *J* stamped on my identity card, just like all other Jews.

My time in hiding would have taken a very different turn: no more school, no more biking, no more going outside—not to mention what would have happened had the Germans found those documents and discovered my hiding place as well. I can't even begin to imagine.

WHAT HAD HAPPENED TO MY SISTER, Freddy Coster, during all that time? It had been forever since I'd seen her. She was often in my thoughts, but as it goes with all memories and reflections on everyday life, I would quickly return to the reality of my immediate situation. I tried to make the best of my time in the countryside, and for that reason tried to ignore any feelings of loss—feelings that would overwhelm me, nevertheless, more often than I wanted.

My parents had sent Freddy to a Catholic girls' boarding school near Brussels fairly soon after realizing that life in the Netherlands was becoming harsher. We had no contact with her. I didn't even know exactly where she was, and I never received a letter from her during my time in hiding—undoubtedly as a safety measure. It turned out later that Freddy had always known where the rest of the family was, myself included, but I don't really know how she'd found out.

In Belgium, she had been in touch with a certain Rabbi Klein, who ministered to American soldiers. One day after the Liberation, my sister decided to return to our parents in Vaassen. She told Rabbi Klein, "Listen, I'll be gone for a while. I'm going to visit my parents."

"Visit your parents?" he asked. "How do you expect to get there?"

"Oh, simple—I'll hitchhike."

"You'll hitchhike? Out of the question," he answered.

A young girl of nineteen hitchhiking right after the Liberation when the country was full of men drunk on the joy of victory, adrenaline in their veins, and looking for an outlet after years of fear and suppression—that was asking for big trouble. Fortunately, the rabbi had his chauffeur drive my sister to Vaassen by truck.

An Unexpected Reunion

During his brief visits to Amsterdam, my father made our apartment habitable again. Although nothing had been looted, time had left its mark: everything was covered with thick, unhealthy layers of dust; the drapes were half-disintegrated; and the acrid smell of rot coming from the kitchen filled every room. That stench suffused the musty, moldy air left after three years of vacancy.

Once the dust had been cleared from the rooms, the drapes replaced, and the house aired out long enough to get rid of the stench, we were able to return to Amsterdam. This was a truly extraordinary outcome—but in a war, extraordinary things aren't all that unusual.

RIGHT AFTER THE WAR, I tried to locate some of my former classmates from the lyceum again, but it was in vain. I couldn't find anyone. I was well aware that untold numbers of people hadn't survived the war. Very possibly, some of them had moved to America in the meantime—something that at the time couldn't be so easily checked. After a while, I abandoned my search, as well as the hope of our ever seeing one another again.

One person I did see after the Liberation was the man with whom I'd gone fishing about a year before: Hendriks, one of the two men from the SS who'd bivouacked at the Van Beeks' house. After the war, that boot polisher appeared at our house in Vaassen, as cool as you please.

He told us what had become of him and his SS colleague just before the Liberation. From Vaassen, they'd ended up near the town of Deventer, where the Germans had a launchpad for V2 rockets intended for London. Apparently, they were filled to the brim with fuel.

His superior, the *Untersturmführer* (second lieutenant), was in dire need of gasoline for his car and ordered, "Hendriks, go get me some of that." Hendriks siphoned off several liters but was caught red-handed by some of the soldiers manning the launchpad. He was immediately thrown in jail where, to his great annoyance, he was surrounded by Dutch Resistance operatives.

That Hendriks was a smooth character. He'd always work things out so shrewdly that, upon reflection, he couldn't possibly be considered trustworthy. Be that as it may, at that point, Hendriks was already convinced that the war was really over. He had no doubt that Germany would get the short end of the stick.

In speaking to the Resistance workers in the prison, he asked, "If I can get you out of here, will you put in a good word for me when the war is over?"

"If you can manage that, we will," they replied.

And he did. How he did it, I have no idea.

He stopped in for coffee to, among other things, tell us that he'd actually rather enjoyed staying with me, my mother, and the Van Beeks. He didn't indicate that he knew we were Jewish—if he'd ever known it at all. If he's still alive today, he probably still doesn't know it.

I never found out what became of his superior.

After the battle near Arnhem in 1944, all the schools were closed, so I only spent a short time in the fourth year of the secondary school in Apeldoorn. The curriculum was divided into A and B courses, and I took the B courses: the technical route. I wanted to be an engineer, for which secondary-school B training was the prerequisite.

After the Liberation, I continued the B courses in Amsterdam where, to my surprise, things were a great deal stricter. I failed geometry. That can't possibly be right, I thought. In that same subject, I'd earned As in Apeldoorn. To my dismay, it turned out to be completely right, and I had to be tutored in algebra and geometry. It turned out that Amsterdam was way ahead of Apeldoorn.

I also discovered that my English was rather poor. Again, I received a failing grade. My education at Nyenrode Business University later rectified that.

In 1946, Nyenrode opened its doors as the Netherlands Training Institute for Foreign Students. In the summer of 1947, when I applied, it already had an excellent reputation. I would be part of the group to attend Nyenrode. There was a great deal of interest in the school: of the twelve hundred applications, only ninety were accepted. I was one of the lucky ones.

It wasn't very difficult to get a scholarship; they were offered by companies involved with the institution. If my memory serves me right, I almost automatically received one of them. But at Nyenrode, I never really had the feeling I was part of the group.

Surprisingly enough, the school that had an important influence on me in terms of my current profession was my elementary school—the Montessori School that Anne Frank also attended. It made me aware of the freedom people have to do what they are best at. One of the important aspects of a Montessori education is perseverance. That school taught us not to easily give up when something doesn't work out right away. However, as a game designer, I have also learned that when something definitely does *not* work, you can and should give up quickly. One example of this is when Ora and I discovered that a game we'd created had already been patented seventeen years before by someone else.

Anne Frank wrote that, the day after Minister Bolkenstein urged people to keep a diary and her housemates heard the news on the radio, they all came rushing at her. Anne ought to use her almost daily entries for a novel about their hiding place, they said. "Just imagine how interesting it would be if I published a novel about the Secret Annex," Anne wrote. It would have to be called *The Secret Annex* for, in her eyes, it was an intriguing title, suggestive of a detective story.

Personally, I'd been totally oblivious to that call by the minister, nor do I know anyone who was immediately inspired to start a diary. As far as I'm aware, there were no diarists around me, or else they didn't discuss it and kept them hidden for the rest of their lives.

Unlike some of my former classmates who were mentioned in Anne's diary, I never had contact with Otto Frank. One day, I purchased a second-run copy of the book. Everyone was talking about it, it got fine reviews, and I was very curious to read what my former classmate had written.

The first time I read it, my name didn't appear yet. Otto Frank had kept many names anonymous when he was preparing the first, as well as the copied, edition. A subsequent edition included most of the actual names.

When I realized Anne was writing about me ("one of my many admirers"), I didn't feel particularly flattered by the comment "he's a rather boring kid," although her opinion of me wasn't bad compared to what she had to say about my cousin Rob Cohen: "Rob Cohen is in love with me, too, but I can't stand him anymore. He is a hypocritical, deceitful, whiny, silly, annoying little boy, who thinks an awful lot of himself."

I got along very well with Rob and didn't think he was full of himself at all—certainly not as much as Anne suggested. His mother was an illustrator, and his whole family made it through the war alive.

To tell the truth, I found the fact that *Anne wrote* more impressive than *what* she wrote. It had surprised me to see how she had emerged as a writer. At the time, none of us realized that she was a writer. For me, the diary contained a lot of very girlish things, and all those fights in the house began to bore me after a while. But then, I wasn't able to imagine her situation very well either: I'd spent my hiding period safely in the country with a very kind foster mother, whereas she had to manage to live with seven other people in a space that was far too small. All the interactions and tensions between them made for a situation entirely different from my own.

A Future in Israel

What my life would ultimately look like in the future may have already been determined in the past.

My paternal grandfather, Grandpa Coster, born in Leeuwarden, was a printer. He moved to Amsterdam where he opened the Coster printing business. He died when I was about six years old, and my father took over the shop. At first, I didn't see much of a future in being a printer. My aim was to go to Delft University of Technology and become a chemical engineer.

After the war, my father ran into financial problems. During the occupation, his printing business had been completely ransacked and destroyed, and he had to start from scratch. Having to pay for six years of university studies didn't exactly appeal to him.

"Just go to the technical college," he told me. One of my classmates from the Montessori School with whom I was still in touch attended Nyenrode and suggested that I go there as well.

After my two years there, I had to do my compulsory military service, where I realized that going into the printing business was perhaps not such a bad idea after all.

Once I was done with the service, I attended the Amsterdam School of Graphics in the Dintelstraat. I completed my training without any trouble, but when I was finished, I felt an urge to see more of the world. The Dutch publisher Arbeiderspers printed *Het Volk* (The People) and had many different departments. For a hundred guilders a month, I was able to do an internship there. I worked in several different departments, including the newspaper's correction department—apparently I was quite good at fixing mistakes at the time. For instance, when a word had been set upside down, I'd notice it right away. (Setting was still done by hand then, and laying out a word upside down was more common than one might think.) They asked if I'd like to work there for a month at full salary. I stayed two months.

Then I left for Sweden for a year. Halfway between Göteborg and Stockholm, I found work at Öberg, a printing business that did conventional as well as specialty printing, including playing cards, printed on three-layered paper (white, black, white). They used gold as well as other colors, and sometimes a single sheet of paper would go through the printer thirteen times. Later on, I spent three months employed by the same company in its branch in Gamla stan, the beautiful Old City of Stockhom.

At that time, my parents had taken my former foster parents on a trip to Belgium. They traveled by car. On a small curvy road with limited visibility, they collided head-on with a car that was passing another vehicle. My father's most serious injury was a complicated thigh fracture. The two women were in the back seat, and both sustained a concussion. Of the group, Barend was in the worst shape: he was partially paralyzed. I had to leave

Sweden at once to become manager of the Coster printing company.

After a convalescence of three years, my father came back, and I became the assistant manager. It seemed preferable to be doing something else. Our company printed the biweekly paper of the Netherlands Zionist Association, *De Joodse wachter* (The Jewish guardian). Jaap Meijer, my former history teacher at the lyceum, was the editor, and I was thrust into the job of technical editor. Because I was a serious young man, I read every single article that appeared in the paper, and so I was well-informed about all that was taking place in Israel. I came to the conclusion that Israelis were good at improvising. It seemed to me to be a fine art to master because I, too, wanted to be good at improvising.

I began looking for a job in Israel and ended up at the state printing office. But it wasn't easy: because it was a foreign enterprise, I needed the permission of Her Majesty Queen Juliana herself. In principle, working for a "foreign government office" was forbidden, but the work I'd be doing there wasn't exactly threatening to the nation. In hindsight, I can say in all good faith that I never put either the queen or the state in any danger.

One of the things I'd learned at the Amsterdam School of Graphics was making price calculations, a skill almost entirely foreign to the Tel Aviv State Printing Office. They asked me to do price calculations at the Jerusalem branch, which was a lot of hard work.

The man titled "the state's printer" enjoyed talking with me to improve his English. After two years of work, it turned out I was too young for a promotion, since those with seniority were advanced first. "But," the state's printer said, "would you mind if I found you another job?"

The very next day, I interviewed at a paper factory. I would do fieldwork trying to solve any problems with our paper. And happily, the position paid twice as much. I crisscrossed the country in a small car, visiting our customers and performing a variety of tasks. The job's one disadvantage was that the company's management was American, which didn't do much for my writing skills in Hebrew.

EARLY ON IN MY STAY in Israel, around 1955, I met a young woman. It was important that I learn Hebrew upon my arrival and as quickly as possible. I worked mornings and devoted myself to my studies in the afternoons, which I did in a kibbutz close to Jerusalem. I'd go there on my moped, and after class, I would explore the surrounding countryside, which is how I discovered—among other things—the impressive ruins of the castle of Godfrey of Bouillon, a famous crusader, and the traces of the ancient Roman road from Jaffa to Jerusalem.

In the kibbutz were two American boys, one of them named Herschel. His foster father, Dov Noj, worked at the printing shop of an Israeli newspaper. Mr. Noj invited us to visit him at work one day. During our visit to his large printing plant, I couldn't keep my mouth shut—after all, I'd already spent a good deal of time in print shops. The employees there were absolutely convinced that anything that came from abroad was superior, and so I was instantly offered the position of technical director. I was still wondering what to do about my Hebrew.

I looked for a place to live in Tel Aviv. In the meantime, I'd already begun to investigate the technical aspects of the business in order to improve it. Since the printing shop was owned by the workers themselves, they were effectively their own boss. Initially, they weren't so keen on being told how things ought to be done by a newcomer, and a foreigner at that.

One night, Mr. Noj threw a party, to which Herschel invited a friend of his named Ora Rosenblat. It was dislike at first sight—until she heard I'd come to Israel on a moped.

The moped I'd had my eye on in the Netherlands was made by Batavus, a company that today only makes bicycles. I'd never ridden one before. When I'd gone to Friesland to pick it up, they had to show me where the gas went and where the brake was. I rode around the square for at least a hundred yards, which I considered to be quite enough practice. After paying, I rode the hundred kilometers (sixty-two miles) back to Amsterdam without stopping.

Riding the moped to Israel had been quite an adventure and certainly an inexpensive way for me to travel. Besides, I'd done about a thousand kilometers (over six hundred miles) by bike in Scandinavia and some long distances in France as well, so I was fairly accustomed to moving about on two wheels in a foreign country. I had an innate desire for adventure that, as far as I can tell, had nothing to do with the war. I spent my nights in a tent in a sleeping bag.

The Dutch automobile association had provided me with a map. It indicated that the road would end between Thessaloníki and Istanbul, which seemed somewhat improbable to me. Surely there would be something, even if it was unpaved. But indeed—the road came to an end and all I saw ahead of me was pastures. A little surprised, nevertheless, I continued along the route I'd planned, across the pastures. Not too long after riding through the sodden grassland, I got stuck. The moped's wheels kept sinking into the mud, and upon closer examination, it turned out that the mud had gotten into my rims. If I were to have kept going, my front or rear tire might well have come off the wheel at any moment—something I couldn't allow to happen in the middle of nowhere.

A passing farmer on the way to his fields saw me and stopped his tractor. Without further ado, he put my moped on his cart, asked where I was heading, and before I could say another word, started the motor of his tractor. That's how I entered Turkey later that same day.

I spent the night in Istanbul where a pen pal of mine lived. Then I continued on to Mersin, a city on the Mediterranean Sea where I intended to rest for a while. But as luck would have it, the Netherlands Company for Harbor Works happened to be building a harbor in Mersin, and I temporarily became warehouse manager in a workers' village. They gave me food, a salary, and amoebic dysentery.

After my recuperation, I took a small ship from Mersin to Haifa where I had a few friends, and from there, I went on to the kibbutz for a so-called kibbutz ulpan: a study kibbutz.

My parents had been fine with my departing for half a year, but to them, the fact that I then wanted to stay in Israel permanently was unforgivable. All the same, I suspect that my life here has been a great deal more interesting than it would have been in the Netherlands. At one point, one of the printing shops for which I worked asked me to design a promotional gift, which took the form of a game. It would be the beginning of a new, unanticipated life for my wife and me.

The Queen's Permission

Usually, changing one's name is an unusual thing to do, but it seemed normal to me at first. When I was at the Van Beeks', it made sense that I'd need a non-Jewish-sounding name to replace Maurice Simon. Besides, I'd never liked that, even before the war, very few people I knew were able to pronounce it properly. Classmates were quick to change it to Morris or Maury. My mother spoke French and, obviously, knew that it was Maurice, but most Dutch people didn't have a clue.

Trying to correct them was hopeless. So I started out feeling negatively about the name. Presented with the opportunity to change that part of myself and, in the bargain, having read a good book whose hero was named Theo clinched the decision for me. But the law required a few additional things.

For decades, my passport had continued to show my old name, and it was on this basis that I acquired an identity card in Israel, although everyone called me Theo. So I went to Tel Aviv's city hall to tell them that I wanted them to add the name Theo. The civil servant was an extremely religious man and not very cooperative. Gruffly, he asked, "What kind of name is Theo supposed to be?"

I answered, "I was one of Anne Frank's classmates." It was neither here nor there, which I knew perfectly well at the time, too, but I'd predicted the effect of the words correctly. He closed his mouth, picked up his pen, and in Hebrew spoke the name Theo out loud, along with the amount of money I owed him.

Fine—so much for my Israeli identity card. There was still my passport, however, which I wanted changed as well. That also turned into a big to-do because, clearly, Her Majesty wouldn't want her subjects to go around changing their identities just like that. I wrote a letter to the minister of justice, explaining why I'd had to assume a different name while in hiding, that even my mother had been obliged to call me by that name, and that after the war it had simply stuck. Finally, Queen Juliana granted her permission via the minister. My passport now reads "Theo Maurice Simon Coster."

Before going to visit my old elementary school with Nanette and Lenie, I mull over our reunion at

Merwedeplein. Though we didn't spend too much time on it, our conversation about the war's effects on the rest of our lives had been quite illuminating. Jacqueline had told us that the war had moved her life into a different direction from what she had originally planned. She had intended to go to the School for Applied Arts to become an interior designer, but in leaving the lyceum to attend the regular school, she'd skipped a year. In the end, when she failed her final exams, she was already nineteen and no longer felt like continuing. She went to England and then to France to learn the languages there. Subsequently, she became a bookbinder and for a while designed book covers, with great success. So, she told us, the war had changed her entire life. Instead of an interior designer, she'd become a bookbinder and then a writer, which was the result of her relationship with Anne. "Because of Anne," she said, "I began to write, not knowing that I had the ability."

Nanette had told us that in the past, her father had envisioned a very different kind of life for her. She felt he'd expected her to go to the university. But when her education at the lyceum was interrupted, it didn't work out. Nanette remarked, "The level of the lyceum must have been extremely high: it's remarkable that, despite everything, I'd mastered enough knowledge at age fourteen to be admitted to the university in Brazil after taking only a few supplementary courses."

I said that was true because when I went to the Christian secondary school in Apeldoorn, I suddenly got As in geometry.

"That wasn't the school, though—that was you," Albert said with a laugh. Then he told us that he'd been in hiding for three years without ever opening a book. Still, after the Liberation, with only the first year at the lyceum under his belt, he was placed in the third year of a secondary school in Hilversum.

Lenie Duyzend had gone to the Vossius Gymnasium after the war—a difficult situation, as she was surrounded by much younger children, as Jacqueline knew. Thereafter, she studied medicine and became a physician.

In a Glass Coffin

A building typical of the thirties, the Montessori School hasn't changed very much. It was renamed and is today the Anne Frank School. Nanette, Lenie, and I carefully scrutinize the edifice. The wall next to the classroom where I spent my elementary school days is exactly the same as it was then. Its surface consists of tiny colored grains of glass, which give a strange sensation when you rub it with your hand.

Memories return automatically—pleasant memories. I remember how we were treated one day to Dutch rusk with aniseed sprinkles because a little princess had been born, who is today the current Queen Beatrix of the Netherlands. And every school throughout the land celebrated the birth in this characteristically Dutch fashion.

What is new is the sign at the school's entrance. It has all the names of all the Jewish pupils who were murdered during the war, the most famous of whom are Anne Frank and her sister, Margot.

Lenie observes how long the list of names is, each name followed by the camp in which the child in question was killed and the date.

"The dates tell you that the children who arrived in Auschwitz and Sobibor were gassed immediately," Nanette says.

"And it shows that Anne Frank died in 1945, right before the Liberation," I say.

"And still there were so many people who died right after the Liberation," Lenie adds. "A teacher I had told me once that if the battle at Arnhem had succeeded, all of Bergen-Belsen would have survived. And I think that's probably true."

"All of Bergen-Belsen?" Nanette seems doubtful.

"Well, a great many, in any event. My uncle and aunt, for instance."

All three of us are thinking the same thing at that moment. We're speculating about the percentage of children in this neighborhood—the River District—that must have been Jewish, and we come up with roughly 20 to 30 percent.

We walk on. The tree in the school yard has grown huge. It takes me some time to find the sandbox. While Nanette and Lenie are talking about their elementary schools (renovated, demolished), a wonderful uproar erupts. The school yard fills with children, laughing and yelling, who cry "old people" in our direction once and then, for no apparent reason, chase after each other or just start shouting.

We look through the window of the kindergarten classroom, then roam through the school for a while. Albert and Jacqueline might have enjoyed coming along as well, but they couldn't make it, unfortunately.

Then again, three is probably just right in front of a class of little children. Four of us would be older than the whole class put together, I think as we enter a classroom.

A friendly teacher greets us, and we introduce ourselves as former classmates of Anne Frank.

"How about that," the teacher says. "What a coincidence, right guys?" She tells us that she and her class have been trying to figure out what Anne Frank would have looked like today.

"Simple: old!" I say, laughing. I notice a small old-fashioned school desk—a little table with a chair attached to it—and I manage to squeeze into it. A perfect fit.

"With gray hair and a few wrinkles, we thought," the teacher says, then asks, "Can we still see her somewhere?"

One of the children gets up. "She's buried in a glass coffin with lots of flowers on top."

"Well, not exactly," Lenie mumbles to herself.

"If that were possible, but we haven't gotten to that part of the lesson yet."

She shows a photograph of Anne on Merwedeplein.

Then I tell them about my time at the school and Anne's birthday party where we watched a film. A small blond boy is avidly picking his nose; he studies the yield with his mouth open, then tastes it with pleasure.

"Which video did you see?" asks a little girl. Apparently, Rin Tin Tin has been replaced by new heroes.

Hannah, a bright little girl with long blond hair, has an urgent question for us.

"Was Anne fun?" she asks, and then more pointedly, "Was she nice?"

"I think so," I answer. "I really wanted to be friends with her. Sometimes we biked to school together—she and I, side by side."

"Because I've also heard she was spunky."

Aha—there's a good word.

"Yes, she certainly had spunk," Lenie says.

"Sometimes she'd talk out of turn," I comment.

"Hey, does that sound familiar?" the teacher asks with a laugh.

THE CLASS THAT FOLLOWS the six-year-olds consists of twelve-year-olds. When we've finished our stories, one boy asks whether we got any funny looks with our yellow stars on our coats.

"No," Nanette answers, "I don't think so. I still have that star. But, of course, it was really awful to be forced to wear it."

"But isn't it horrible to see that star again now? Doesn't it make you feel terrible? Doesn't it make you think about everything all over again?" a girl asks.

"Sure, but it's more than just the star alone," Nanette says. Before she can say anything else, other questions follow each other at a rapid pace: Did she ever have anything to do with the Germans in her own house? Did Anne have many friends? What did I think of Anne's diary? What was the most cherished thing that had been taken from Nanette as a Jew?

"My freedom," Nanette answers right away. When they hear that she was in a concentration camp, the children want to know everything about her. She tells them that in Bergen-Belsen, she tried to avoid the labor as best she could. She was young and repeatedly had to repair the outer walls of the barracks in the freezing cold, but other than that, she had never been made to work the outdoor shifts.

When we're back outside, all three of us are almost dizzy from the myriad of questions the children have fired at us.

Nanette and I say good-bye to Lenie, whom I'll see again the next day, and then find a bench in the sun where we can talk quietly. I know she'd been extremely ill right after the Liberation, and I'm interested in hearing how she managed to keep going during that period. I ask what happened when she returned to the Netherlands after the war.

"I came back from Germany by plane. At the time, the Royal Air Force was transporting a small group of girls whose health left something to be desired. As I see it, they must have thought we wouldn't survive a train trip. We arrived in Eindhoven, where we were cared for in a school that had been turned into a reception center. From there, I was sent to the Sanatorium Brederodeduin Santpoort, part of an insane asylum that had been set up as a sanatorium. I was there for three years until I was finally allowed to leave in May 1948. Then I stayed with a former nurse of my brother's in Bennekom, on the estate of a castle in the middle of the woods. I had to rest, and couldn't be up for more than two hours in the morning and the afternoon. At last, the day came when they said I'd recovered and could start living a normal life. In December 1946, I'd already visited London once for six weeks to see family, and then in April 1949, I went to live there permanently."

I ask Nanette if Otto Frank had looked her up as well. After the war, Anne's father had gone to see several of Anne's friends to talk about his daughter, about earlier times, and about the diary, too. She explains that the Red Cross had provided Otto Frank with a list of the names of all those who had survived the camps, which is how he found out that Nanette was among them.

"He wrote me a letter, and I answered him saying I'd seen Anne in Bergen-Belsen, probably in February 1945. I saw her through the barbed wire the first time, when the camps still had separate sections, but that wire was removed later on. Since I knew she was there, I went looking for her. That's when she told me she'd continued writing in her diary during her time underground and that she wanted to use it to write a book when the war was over. I don't know how she could've known the diary still existed.

"I also wrote Otto that in the sanatorium I'd met a girl who'd been in the camps with Anne and Margot. I mentioned that I didn't think they'd gone from Westerbork to Auschwitz together but that somehow or another they'd met up again later. I also let him know that it was she who'd told his daughters that their mother had survived the selection process."

Shortly thereafter, Otto Frank came to see Nanette, at which time he told her that he was considering having Anne's diary published. His mother, who was living in Switzerland, thought it was a good idea.

"Otto asked me how I felt about that," Nanette says. "I was sixteen; what did I know? I said, 'If you think it's a good idea, then I would do it.'"

Otto sent Nanette the first copy, printed on the cheap paper that was the norm then. She loaned it out and never got it back, she says regretfully.

I ask what she thought of the book when she first read it.

"My reaction may surprise you." Nanette hesitates. "I'm from that same time and had many of the same experiences as she, so for me it wasn't all that spectacular. We were accustomed to such events, so it didn't have the same impact on me as it did on so many other people. I could never have imagined then that after the Bible, it would become the second most widely read book in the world."

"What do you think of the reputation it's gained over the course of the years?"

Nanette searches for her words. "In some way, the book has promoted the myth that for so long struck such a sympathetic chord in the Netherlands—namely, the myth that the Dutch had helped their Jewish compatriots. This is actually contradicted by the number of those who died; about 80 percent of the Jewish minority in the Netherlands was killed during the war. I don't believe that's the percentage that would have died had everyone been as great as we've been told."

In countries such as Belgium and France, the figure was apparently half of that. Whether the dramatic difference in the Netherlands can be blamed on a less helpful population is hard to say. In the early days of the war, France and Belgium had an escape route to the south, which the Netherlands lacked, and that may have played a role. Furthermore, Belgium and France just had a German military government. The Netherlands had not only a Nazi military government but a Nazi civil administration as well, which meant that the anti-Jewish threat was omnipresent. All the same, it doesn't take much for that high percentage of Jewish victims—four out of every five—to disgust you, even now.

When Nanette returned from the war, she was too ill to be angry, she says. But she did suffer.

"I kept wondering why I had survived when so many others had died. It was extremely difficult to accept the fact that besides me, no one in my family had made it through."

At first, Nanette didn't know what had happened to her parents. She had dreams of her father in which he pointed out a direction for her to take while the rest of the family headed down a different path. She suspects she knew subconsciously that there was no one else left, for in the end, everyone in her family was gone.

"My parents, my brother, cousins . . ." Nanette fixes her gaze ahead. "My father died on November 4th, 1944. I assume that in the exchange process, he was the most important one of our family. After him, the Germans were unlikely to be terribly interested in the rest of us. My brother was deported to Oranienburg on December 4th, and on the fifth, my mother left for Beendorf. She worked in a factory there, five hundred or six hundred meters (nearly two thousand feet) under the ground where, together with other foreign prisoners, she made airplane parts. The conditions were atrocious. However, she still made one more train trip, from Beendorf to Hamburg, and from there on to Sweden. On that trip, she died." It was right before the Liberation.

"Do you remember the last time you saw her?"

"Yes, it was that same December 5th, 1944, in Bergen-Belsen, when they ripped her away from me."

Nanette was the only one who remained. The war had made her into an orphan at age fifteen. When there's no one else, you have to learn to take care of yourself. She believes this changed her as a person.

After the Liberation, the Dutch bureaucracy returned as if it had never left. It established rules and regulations that weren't helpful to the camp survivors in any way whatsoever.

"When I was sick, it turned out that the authorities had frozen my bank account," Nanette says. "I could challenge it, but they made it clear to me that my chances of winning the case were zero. My family in England was able to come to my aid. It so happened that there was an international rationing system whereby coupons could be traded for postage stamps. My family in England sent me those coupons, and in spite of my illness, I managed to make a deal with the post office where I could exchange them there for cash instead of stamps. A completely absurd situation. In the end, the Amsterdam Bank did help me to get my money back.

"Another regulation that was bad rather than favorable for those who'd been in hiding or arrested was this: if parents hadn't come to pick up their children within a month, they wouldn't be able to get custody of them again until they'd been declared mentally competent. That rule was actually applied!"

At the time, Nanette knew nothing about this law, but her family in England did and had become quite worried that they wouldn't be able to get their niece back. She herself didn't hear about it until 1991 when the Symposium of the Hidden Child was organized. It was only then that she understood why her family had become "so neurotic," as she puts it.

"I spoke to a psychiatrist once," Nanette says. "He said to me, 'If you've made it through everything that's happened to you, you don't need a psychiatrist to tell you what to do.'" She laughs.

"But did you really not need any therapy or counseling after the war?" I ask.

"Well, there wasn't anything like that then. Perhaps I could have used it, but I don't know what I'd be like today if I had been in therapy. I didn't talk about it in England. One of my cousins asked me once if I wouldn't like to know what I said in my sleep. But

I didn't. It was only with fellow victims that I was able to talk about my experiences. In London, I just couldn't."

In Love in London

It was in London, at the end of a Zionist meeting, that Nanette met her future husband. It was actually lucky that she wasn't very familiar with the area, she says.

"When the meeting was over, I heard a few of the participants say they were going back to the Golders Green Bus Station. I wasn't sure how to get home, but from that point on, I'd be fine. So I turned around and asked, 'If you're going to Golders Green Station, can I come along?'

"A young man looked at me and said, 'Miss, I'll take you there and put you on the bus myself.'

"That was John. He'd already noticed me—noticed that I was alone. A thin, lonely young woman in a blue summer dress.

"'Do you have a boyfriend?' he asked once we were seated.

"'No,' I said.

"'Okay, well . . . you aren't really my type.'

"He told me later that it had been a defense mechanism on his part and at that very moment, he'd resolved that if he ever saw me again he would marry me. And one week later, still in London, a city of millions, our paths crossed again. He was coming down a street as I was walking up.

"'Hey, aren't you the girl I put on the bus last week?' he called out.

"'Yes, and thanks again,' I called back. 'Bye.'

"I continued on my way. But apparently, he'd made his decision and took action. When he came home, he asked a friend, with whom he'd gone to the meeting, who else had been there that day. That's how he found out my name. And my telephone number.

"He asked if I would like to go to a concert with him that Friday during our first phone conversation. I told him that no one in our family goes out on Friday nights. Then he called me at work, and this time I told him I was busy and couldn't talk to him.

"He said, 'I have tickets for a concert'—which wasn't true at all, by the way. After that call, I phoned my aunt. 'That guy called me again. What should I do now?'

"What I didn't know was that she'd already checked him out. Apparently, she thought things looked all right and said, 'Why not go out with him this once, and if you don't like him, you can always drop him.'

"John called again. I told him calmly that I worked in the center of London, for the Bank of England, but then suddenly I couldn't stop myself and quickly said I'd meet him in front of the bank. That's how it all began."

Nanette describes how John had come to England with his cousin. His parents had both died of cancer many years before. That cousin was John's witness at the wedding.

"Just as I was about to enter the synagogue, I suddenly realized that no one in my family would be there for me. Why should I really get married? I wondered. Why start a family? What will become of my children? Will the same fate be in store for them as for all the Jewish children who ended up in the gas chambers?"

It was only when she saw her husband-to-be standing there that she had the courage to keep going. Later, they moved to Brazil to be near John's family, and that's where they've been for more than fifty years now.

"We have five grandchildren and one great-grandchild. I can show them old family photos. It's a small miracle that I still have them, because the Germans should have taken everything when they emptied our house out, but they forgot one box, and that happened to be the box with photographs. The neighbors picked it up off the floor and saved it all those years."

"Did you ever consider going back to the Netherlands?" I ask cautiously.

"No," she answers without hesitation. "Because of everything that happened here. It doesn't appeal to me." I can well imagine it. Nanette had been through enough here: problems leaving the sanatorium, problems leaving the Netherlands. Besides, John had family in Brazil, and why should he move to such an unfamiliar country?

A Grim Message

Jacqueline remembers the Liberation not just as a huge relief but also as a turning point in her life when she had to absorb tragic news. Her dear friend Anne, whom she thought had been safely living in Switzerland for years, turned out not to have survived the war. It was Otto's unhappy task to have to inform her.

"The very first time Otto Frank came to see us, I was astonished that he came alone," Jacqueline began. "Where was Anne? I never worried about her for a second during the war; I was so sure she was in Switzerland. So when he stood there before us, thin as a rail and so sad, I didn't get it. Then he told us they'd never left for Switzerland but had been in hiding in the Secret Annex on the Prinsengracht.

"'We were betrayed and taken away,' he said. 'My wife is dead—she died in Auschwitz. I know nothing about Anne and Margot. I hope they're still alive.'

"From then on, people were intermittently returning from the camps, and he'd ask them if they'd seen his children. This went on for weeks until he came in contact with two sisters in Rotterdam who told him, 'We saw them, and we watched them die.'

"After that first time, he stopped by more frequently. Not long ago, I was wondering if he actually came by as often as I remembered, and then I had the chance to flip through his diaries—his small date books. He did visit us often—sometimes twice a week. Then he'd take me out because he didn't want to talk about Anne at my house. As soon as he saw me, he'd start weeping again. Every single time. He was absolutely inconsolable, of course. The woman who'd given him the news said later on, 'It was so hard for me to have to tell a father that his daughters are dead—a father who was still hoping to see them alive.' He suffered deeply, and I found it very difficult to watch. At one point, he took me to the Annex, before it ever became a museum. People sometimes ask me if it didn't make me think of Anne the whole time I was there, but strange as it may sound, I was too preoccupied with him, how he was feeling about having been in hiding there with his whole family and now being the only one left. At that moment, that bothered me far more.

"It didn't become truly emotional for me until much later when Otto showed me the original letters Anne had written me and then copied in her diary—because she couldn't send them. I received a typed copy of those letters the first time, and that was overwhelming enough in itself. I was truly and deeply moved in 1970, when I was allowed to see the diary, which Otto had taken from the safe for the occasion.

"In her letters to me, Anne was optimistic. She assumed the war would be over soon.

"I think she was happy that she could entrust anything to her diary. I gather she was pretty lonely among all those adults. It must have been her reason for inventing a letter I supposedly wrote to her—and I thought that was really awfully sad. She also wrote letters to imaginary friends, just to have some companionship, so I do believe she was incredibly lonely.

"On the other hand, Anne did want to become famous, as she writes in her diary as well. It is consistent with her character, too, I think: she did see herself as the center of the world—just as she also believed at the time that all kinds of boys in her class were in love with her. I'd never really noticed it, but that could be me, too. Later, I talked with several boys from that class who had survived—Rob Cohen, for example—who said, 'Oh, Anne thought that every boy was in love with her.' I think she truly believed it herself because, in my opinion, she wrote her diary in complete honesty. Of course, the boys must have liked her because she was funny and fun to be with.

"Hello was a boy with whom she'd take occasional walks. Her girlfriends would see that, of course, and Anne in turn would find that exciting. She'd glance at us to see if we were still watching. In a TV interview, I heard Hello mention that he was actually in love with Margot but that she was completely unapproachable. He did think Anne was fun."

"And was Anne in love with anyone?" I ask Jacqueline.

"I don't think so."

"And you?"

"Me? Well, there was a boy I really liked, but he didn't come back from the war. He once gave me a bracelet, which I've always kept. Jopie de Beer was his name." She laughs. "But really in love? God, I was only twelve, thirteen. I don't know. I found him quite fascinating."

"What would Anne say if she knew you're writing and giving lectures about her now?"

"I'm frequently asked to speak in Germany. That's particularly interesting for me because the audience there is very attentive. I enjoy talking about the era, and they listen to me because I'm talking about Anne. Anne would have been thrilled with all of it—all that attention for her. That it's hers now, and that her hiding place is named for her, and that everyone in the whole world knows her, she would have loved it.

"There was a girl once who asked me what Anne would think of everything I now do. It took me a long time to come up with the answer, but I think she'd be very happy with what I'm doing. Amazed but happy."

Levels of Suffering

While I learned about the Liberation indirectly via the sound of a motorcycle, Albert heard it on the radio. "At my last hiding place, I'd learned how to make crystal receivers," he says, "so I could listen to the English station by myself. One night, they broadcast the news that the Germans had surrendered. Together with a great many other people in Eemnes, my father went out into the street. Supposedly, that's when his shoes were ruined—totally irreplaceable possessions during the occupation." Albert describes it as if he doesn't entirely trust the symbolic coincidence—whether it's true or not, it makes for a good story, of course.

"Two days after we heard about the German surrender, the Americans and British entered our village. In that one-day interval, we still had Germans checking ID papers in front of our door, so even the day after the Liberation, we were still afraid to leave the house: they might well have shot us on the spot.

"After the war, I went back to school in Hilversum. At lunchtime, I was surrounded by kids who'd been through the war but without experiencing three years of persecution. That's when the realization really hit me hard that I'd been forced to spend a number of years under exceptionally horrifying circumstances. I'd lost virtually my entire family, I was living in a strange place, had spent three years in mortal danger, and couldn't share any of it with anyone. That first new school day was really dismal for me.

"Only about fifteen years ago they organized a conference in Amsterdam for the children in hiding, where those who'd been children when they went underground could share their stories. Until then, the prevailing view was that if you'd gone into hiding, you hadn't really experienced anything because the camps were far worse. And even at the conference, that feeling didn't really leave me: I may have been in hiding, but it was with my father, mother, and sister, and all four of us came out alive. Most of the others in attendance had all been dropped off by their parents somewhere, and many of those parents were murdered, so they miss them or miss their brothers and sisters. Compared to other children in hiding, I don't think my story amounts to much. What happened to me wasn't all that bad, was it? Three years in hiding with the family and all four of us surviving . . . isn't that splendid?

"But that's not really how it works at all—that one form of suffering is worse than another. It's not true; it's all a matter of each individual's personal experience, and yet that's how they were handling it: the worst thing was to have been in a camp; next was that of the child from a large family who'd been in hiding and separated from them, and then came back on his or her own; and a situation such as ours, well, that wasn't terribly serious, even we ourselves agreed. And yet, I'd lost three-quarters of my family.

"We didn't discuss it much. A few years later—I'm now going back to about 1947—when we'd returned to Amsterdam, there were some other Jewish students in my class, but we never spoke about what had happened to us. Not until many years later did I have a conversation with a woman who'd been in my class. Her family situation was terribly tragic, but at the time, I never knew anything about it. It simply wasn't discussed."

The Importance of Blond Hair

Elburg, the little town where Lenie Duyzend had spent her final time underground, was liberated on April 19. Contrary to what I expected, we don't talk about feelings of happiness but rather about family members who didn't survive, about the difficulties of going underground and the many betrayals that cost so many Jews their lives.

"My grandmother was murdered or died in the train to Auschwitz," Lenie says. "And one of my mother's sisters was killed with her husband and four children in Sobibor. The parents of one of my cousins were put to death, also in Sobibor, as was one of my mother's brothers with his wife and small son.

"In 1941, when every Jew had to register and provide all the information about their origin, many people did. Subsequently, it became known that of those Jews who hadn't done so, many had survived the war. So, large numbers of us were registered with full names and complete addresses. And many really looked Jewish as well, even without a star, so just by walking down the street you were already putting yourself in jeopardy. My parents were in two separate hiding places. My father had to stay inside because he looked Jewish, but my mother could go out because she was blond and could pass.

"The terrible thing, of course, was that the better part of the Dutch population was indifferent, and a great many people, insofar as their family situation would have permitted it, just didn't dare take Jews into their home. Before I ended up in Elburg, I spent a few days with a different family: a husband and wife with a two-year-old child. The woman was very pregnant and didn't want to take it on—understandably. Just a few days later, I moved in with the other family."

"Do you feel as if you lost part of your youth?"

"A part of it, yes. There were strict limitations while in hiding and therefore very little contact with the outside. When I arrived at the underground camp, there was some contact, at least—mostly with Jews. It was nice to be able to talk with fellow sufferers and not be locked up by myself anymore. All in all, I was in hiding for a little less than two years. Every time betrayal seemed imminent, I was somehow lucky enough to escape. The informers were paid; and sometimes it was a matter of carelessness on the part of those in hiding, or of those who were hiding them as well, perhaps. In any event, many people were betrayed. One-third seems to be the official figure, but I believe that half of the Jews who went underground were betrayed."

We fall silent. I wonder why Lenie was informed on so frequently—did it have to do with the size of the camp where she was? Once again, I consider myself rather lucky: the teacher's nephew from Amsterdam who didn't have to have a *J* stamped on his ID card. For me, it was relatively easy to keep my identity concealed—and when they don't know who you are, there's nothing to betray.

epilogue

I ring the doorbell of my former hiding place in Vaassen and wonder whether the current residents will be able to help me reconstruct my past. The chance that they would have known me is minimal, but they might know someone else who also lived here during the war. Next to the front door is a bouquet of dried flowers in a frame of pinecones.

A cheerful woman opens the door. Her seventy-three-year-old husband is in and speaks with me. They bought the house from the Van Beeks in 1966 and made a lot of alterations during the seventies. The school next door is long gone.

The man remembers me very faintly when I remind him that I used to pass as the teacher's nephew. "But it's hard, you see, because of the beard you now have. Or did you already have that when you were thirteen?"

I ask if he still knows anyone from that time—and he does. Unlike my own, his memory is still very good. Together we come up with some names but no new ones that I recognize. Besides, each and every one of them is now dead.

We observe repeatedly how long it's been since that time. A complete historiography of the war seems absolutely impossible when I reflect on how difficult it is just to unearth details about my own past. I ask again if he knows anyone else who could possibly remember me.

"I do have a few in mind, but they're all gone," he says.

"But of course, darling," his wife says, "Teuntje Beekhuis."

"That's true—Teuntje Beekhuis. Do you remember her?"

For a moment I draw a blank. "Not really. Maybe a little. Of course, it's sixty years ago for me as well. Does she live far away?"

"No, very close. In assisted living. I'm sure you'll be able to see her."

MRS. T. BEEKHUIS IT SAYS on the doorbell panel. As soon as I explain why I'm here, the door opens. The elevator takes me to a hallway with several doors. A woman opens one with a smile. "You don't recognize me, do you?" she says.

It didn't take her long to notice that.

"Not immediately," I say, "but it's good to see you again."

"For me, too. I still remember you as a boy." She holds out her hands indicating how short I was then. She invites me inside her home and introduces her niece, Betty Vos, to me, a lady with long strings of beads and the bearing of a 1950s movie star.

"What are you actually here for?" Teuntje asks. I explain that I'm simply hoping to find someone who used to know me when I was in hiding and can perhaps enlighten me a little about that time.

"We were living in the Julianalaan throughout the war. A Jewish couple was hiding there as well." She adds that Betty, her niece, shared the room with the couple. When visitors came, she'd very quickly close the door.

"I'm almost afraid to ask," I say. "I'm seventy-eight. And how young are you?"

"Eighty-four next month. So, a lot older than you." She laughs.

She tells me that she'd seen me at the funeral of either Mr. or Mrs. Van Beek but that we hadn't spoken then.

"That's when I told Betty, 'Well, that's not Theo anymore; he's changed so much.' You had a beard, and I only knew you as a boy, of course. Easygoing, a jumper. I don't know if you were a member of a club or something like that. Anyway, there weren't many clubs during the war."

I tell her about our little glider plane club and about the work I now do, designing games—maybe her children played with one of them at some time. When I tell her that I stayed with the Van Beeks until the end of the war, Teuntje says that it had been a risky undertaking, considering I was attending school. She adds that they had people hiding in their house as well, among whom was a Jewish woman, Mrs. Van Tijn, who used to go to Amsterdam to visit a family member and collect money for the shopping needs of those in hiding. Teuntje's sister would accompany Mrs. Van Tijn on the train to Amsterdam.

"But even today, my sister will say that she can't understand why our mother ever allowed her to go to Amsterdam to help her collect that money. And I'm still not sure how much money they had to pay for boarding. In any case, I don't think it could have been very much."

"If my memory serves me right, my mother came every month to pay the Van Deelen family sixty-five guilders, I believe. That was the room and board for the Van Beeks, but I have the feeling they would have done it even if they hadn't been paid. I often say that my parents gave me life but that the Van Beeks kept me alive."

"I don't recall how it was with us. Anyhow, there came a point when those in hiding couldn't get any more money. Thereafter, it was all done in good faith, and they would reimburse the full amount after the war. We kept in touch until the end; and they attended my brother's and sister's weddings, too."

"Were they able to go around freely in Vaassen?"

"No—a short distance to visit another family, but only in the evening after dark. Other than that, they didn't go out. They were supposed to stay with us for just three weeks, and then they'd move on to an address in Emst. All of us thought the war would be over soon. My father used to say that our house was elastic: you could cram a lot in. We'd made a shelter where they could hide in the daytime during raids.

"We had a radio, too, that members of the Resistance would come and listen to. It sat on the landing and so those who were hiding in my room were listening as well, unbeknownst to the Resistance members. You can't betray what you don't know.

"Before the arrival of the people we hid, the drapes in front were always open and we had lots of flowers on the windowsills. When they moved in, the drapes were drawn and the flowers disappeared. If anyone asked us the reason for the austerity, we'd say that we no longer had any money for flowers. A close friend of mine who used to visit every other week never asked a single question—even though we were hiding people for two years and three months. It was much better not to ask anything."

"Did you know any collaborators in this area?"

"Yes—Witteveen of the Geelmolen estate. But you must know that."

"No."

"He was the head of the NSB here in Vaassen, but a fine farmer. He worked at the Geelmolen, that large estate here, and his children were always dressed in black and wore a small orange cap. Sometimes they passed our house on the Julianalaan on their bikes. He did show mercy to a few people, but he was a true NSB man. They used to go to church with us, but when they joined the NSB, they apparently lost touch with the minister. They lived next door to us, which is why my father looked them up once after the war. Witteveen felt that the church had abandoned him: although he was the one who'd stopped going to church, he felt that the church should have sought contact with him."

"Were there any other Jews in Vaassen?"

"Oh yes—Mr. and Mrs. Van den Bosch, but you never knew that. They were in hiding as well but would secretly visit us now and then."

It gives me great pleasure to tell her that the Van Beek family not only considered me their child but had truly loved me. And I adored that.

"True. You belonged in every way. You went to school normally, on your bike. You really were their son—and everything that goes with it."

"Did you have any idea at the time that I was Jewish?"

"Not just an idea—I knew it!" she answers with a smile.

"What?" I think I've misunderstood her. "You knew it?"

"It was common knowledge. No one knew that we were hiding a Jewish couple, but everyone knew about the Van Beeks. But it wasn't discussed."

It's a while before I can utter a word.

ONCE OUTSIDE, I'M STILL in shock. I didn't have any inkling that people knew about me. I assumed that I was simply accepted as the teacher's nephew. And now it turns out that the whole village knew I was Jewish and that they all kept it a secret.

This was a complete surprise. Had I known that I wasn't riding around quite as anonymously as I thought, my entire time in hiding would have been very different. I would have been terrified every minute of the day, I'm sure, and the things I look back on with relative pleasure now (going to school, riding my bike, making model planes) would have been utterly inconceivable. Like Albert and Lenie, I would have had to stay out of sight at all times and move from one hiding place to another—or remain in a single location like Anne, behind windows nailed shut, completely closed off from the outside world.

I reflect on how easily good fortune can turn to bad luck. What if Barend van Beek had been an unpopular, rather than a respected, headmaster, with whom some of the villagers had a bone to pick? Would I still be here today? What if the nameless civil servant who processed my papers of origin had decided I had not two but four Jewish grandparents? In my case, things always worked out for the best—and who knows? I may have been lucky in other ways I'm not even aware of. But by the same token, things could also have taken a very different turn for me. Anne Frank's father had planned his family's concealment down to the last detail, but the good fortune that was so frequently on my side deserted them that one time only.

Good fortune and bad luck ought not to play such important roles in one's life. They may be essential to winning a game, but as soon as lives depend on them, there is no justice. That was all too often the case in World War II—and in every other war as well, of course.

It seems there's little awareness today of what it truly means to live during wartime, and of the importance of preventing wars. It is something that requires constant reflection.

the film

After one of the most extraordinary weeks of my life, my small film crew and I boarded the plane for Tel Aviv at Amsterdam's Schiphol Airport. Our carry-on luggage contained the film footage—eighteen reels, eighty minutes each. The experience had already affected me profoundly, but it wasn't about me; it was about leaving something behind—something tangible (an inheritance in cinematic form) so that the generations after mine may have some idea of what a child's life in wartime is like: the everyday and the exceptional, the small moments of happiness and the unbelievable suffering, the cruel fickleness of fate.

On a beautiful day in March 2008, the moment had finally arrived: the documentary *The Classmates of Anne Frank* was complete. The first audience to see the film, as I had always intended, consisted of my grandchildren. And, of course, the classmates themselves immediately received copies. They assured me that a year and a half of emailing, writing, and filming had not been done in vain.

The film was shown publicly for the first time at the Tel Aviv Cinematheque and then, in subsequent months, at various film festivals in Jerusalem, Bucharest, Berlin, Paris, São Paulo, and New York. I was invited for a screening in Montreal and afterwards in Edmonton, later in April 2009, it won the Silver Ace Award at the Las Vegas International Film Festival. That same month, it was shown on television in Israel, and in the spring of 2010, it was shown on Dutch television. It is my hope that both in the Netherlands and wherever else the film may appear, it will contribute to a better understanding of the personal history of children in wartime. They should never be victims of the hatred and intolerance of adults.

bibliography

Barnouw, David, and Gerrold van der Stroom, eds. *De dagboeken van Anne Frank* [The diaries of Anne Frank]. Amsterdam: 2001.

Frank, Anne. *Het Achterhuis: Dagboekbrieven 12 Juni 1942 1 Augustus 1944* [The Secret Annex: Diary letters 12 June 1942–1 August 1944]. Amsterdam: 2008.

Frank, Anne. *Verhaaltjes, en gebeurtenissen uit het Achterhuis: Cady's leven* [Tales from the Secret Annex: Including her unfinished novel Cady's Life]. Uitgeverij Bert Bakker, Amsterdam: 2001.

Gold, Alison Leslie. *Hannah Goslar Remembers: A Childhood Friend of Anne Frank.* New York: 1997.

Herzberg, Abel J., *Kroniek der Jodenvervolging, 1940–1945* [Chronicle of the persecution of the Jews, 1940–1945]. Amsterdam: 1985.

Hondius, Dienke. *Absent: Herinneringen aan het Joods Lyceum Amsterdam, 1941–1943* [Memories of the Jewish Lyceum Amsterdam, 1941–1943]. Amsterdam: 2001.

Lee, Carol Ann. *Anne Frank, 1929–1945: Het leven van een jong meisje—De definitieve biografie* [Anne Frank, 1929–1945: The life of a young girl—The definitive biography]. Amsterdam: 2009.

Liempt, Ad van. *Kopgeld: Nederlandse premiejagers op zoek naar Joden* [Reward money: Dutch bounty hunters in search of Jews]. Amsterdam: 2002.

Lindwer, Willy. *De laatste zeven maanden van Anne Frank: Het ongeschreven laatste hoofdstuk van het dagboek* [Anne Frank's last seven months: The unwritten chapter of the diary]. Hilversum: 2008.

Maarsen, Jacqueline van. *Anne en Jopie: Leven met Anne Frank* [Anne and Jopie: Life with Anne Frank]. Amsterdam: 1990.

Maarsen, Jacqueline van. *Ik heet Anne, zei ze, Anne Frank* [My name is Anne, she said, Anne Frank]. Uitgeverij Marten Muntinga bv.Amsterdam: 2003.

Metselaar, Menno, Ruud van der Rol, Dineke Stam, and Hansje Galesloot, eds. *Anne Frank Huis: Een museum met een verhaal* [Anne Frank House: A museum with a story]. Amsterdam: Anne Frank Foundation, 2008.

Müller, Melissa. *Anne Frank. De biografie* [Anne Frank: The biography]. Amsterdam: 1998.

Presser, Dr. J. *Ondergang: De vervolging en verdelging van het Nederlandse Jodendom, 1940–1945* [Perdition: The persecution and extermination of Dutch Jewry]. Den Haag[u14]: 1965.

Visser, A. *Het verscholen dorp: Verzet en onderduikers op de Veluwe* [The hidden village: Resistance and those in hiding on the Veluwe]. Bredewold-Wezep: 2000.

index